MW00529151

Bottom-Line SELLING

The Sales Professional's Guide to Improving Customer Profits

JACK MALCOLM

CB

CONTEMPORARY BOOKS

Library of Congress Cataloging-in-Publication Data

Malcolm, Jack.
    Bottom-line selling / Jack Malcolm.
       p. cm.
    ISBN 0-8092-2852-1
    1. Selling.   I. Title.
    HF5438.25.M326 1999
    658.85—dc21   98-22489
                                        CIP

Interior design by Maryland Composition Company, Inc.

Published by Contemporary Books
A division of NTC/Contemporary Publishing Group, Inc.
4255 West Touhy Avenue, Lincolnwood (Chicago), Illinois 60646-1975 U.S.A.
Printed in the United States of America
International Standard Book Number: 0-8092-2852-1
99 00 01 02 03 04 QP 18 17 16 15 14 13 12 11 10 9 8 7 6 5 4 3 2 1

Contents

Part 1

Introduction

1

Selling in Changing Times

May you live in interesting times.

Ancient Chinese curse

Whether or not you consider it a curse or a blessing, the times that we live in are certainly interesting. For about the last dozen years, we have been riding a wave of change that shows no sign of breaking anytime soon. The events since roughly the mid-1980s have been dramatic, sudden, and unexpected. And the pace of change is, if anything, accelerating. Who knows what the next 10 years will bring? As Churchill said, "I never make predictions, especially about the future."

Probably the most dramatic upheaval has occurred in the international political scene, but equally momentous domestic changes have taken place that have translated directly into everyday changes here at home. Our society, our culture, our schools, our economy—in fact, all of our institutions—have seen dramatic shifts in the old order. Long-established ways of looking at the world around us and of doing things are yielding to new pressures and imperatives, and quickening change seems to be the only constant.

Our economy and business culture have been affected as dramatically as any other sector of society. Corporate America has undergone wrenching changes over the past decade. The commercial landscape is littered with the names of once proud players who have fallen by

3

the wayside. Names once synonymous with business greatness are remembered only in case studies as examples to be avoided. Millions of middle managers have added sudden unemployment to their midlife burdens and have had to painfully start over either as independents or in unfamiliar new careers.

Two conspicuous trends have converged in the stream of economic history to produce these changes: the unprecedented pace of technological improvement and the globalization of the economy. Technology has made previously undreamed-of improvements in productivity and competitiveness possible; globalization has made them necessary. In some cases the combination of the two has caused revolutionary changes in business practices.

TECHNOLOGY

A central characteristic of human know-how is that, unlike a genie, once it has been let out of the bottle, it can't be put back in. Firms raise the ante by introducing new and better ways to do things, only to find that their competitive advantage lasts just as long as it takes their rivals to figure out how to do it better, cheaper, or faster—and so the cycle continues. Your customers and prospects are playing competitive leapfrog, facing an endless cycle of escalating expectations, in which winning an advantage today earns them only an entry to tomorrow's even tougher game.

For example, the overnight-delivery industry did not even exist 25 years ago. When Federal Express promised to guarantee delivery of packages overnight, the market was skeptical at best. Beginning with the first flight which delivered only three packages, the industry rapidly took off. Competitors quickly joined the contest. Soon it was not good enough just to get the package there overnight with almost perfect success; the package delivery company also had to be able to instantly tell the consumer exactly where the package was when asked. The next step was order fulfillment: the company not only delivers but even assembles customers' products for them. As of this writing, FedEx now supplies software that allows its customers to track packages themselves. Where will it end?

The Federal Express experience points out that competitive advantage is ephemeral: today's dazzling new capabilities are tomorrow's price of admission to the competition. The bar is always being raised for your customers, and their own customers' initial delight at the new level of value quickly becomes "What have you done for me lately?"

Technology has also significantly lowered barriers to entry, expanding the pool of likely competitors. As computing power grows ever cheaper and more accessible, "high tech" is almost a superfluous term: the technology is accessible to anyone.

Information technology is transforming marketing from a mass phenomenon to "mass customization." This phrase, which might have been an oxymoron a few years ago, simply means that information technology gives firms the flexibility to quickly adapt their product to fit individual customer needs, and their customers come to expect it.

GLOBALIZATION

The globalization of the economy, caused partly by the new technologies, has in turn stimulated even faster change. National sovereignty, distance, and protected markets are crumbling against the onslaught of computerization and communications, to name just two of the technologies. Manufacturing firms are being exposed to the full force of international competition, and knowledge and services, which are becoming primary in the world economy, are even less affected by borders and geographic barriers.

Gone forever are the comfortable days when businesses in other countries could be relied on to "know their place" and compete only in commodities and low-tech industries. No country has a corner on brains and innovation, so the marketplace is getting ever more crowded. The net effect is that the pool is bigger, and there are some big and swift fish out there competing for the same food supply.

EVOLUTION AND REVOLUTION

Technology often has consequences unintended by its creators. When you combine that factor with intense competitive pressure, surprising things can happen. Driven by human ingenuity and need, technology acquires a momentum of its own, and incremental improvements give way to revolutionary methods and goals. Many companies have invested in technology to automate existing processes, only to find out that technological improvements have permitted radically different ways of doing things. Rather than automating the steps, they have found ways to totally eliminate them.

Although technological improvements can often provide unexpected benefits, sometimes the opposite can happen. Some technologies offer elegant solutions when the public just does not perceive a problem. As of this writing, personal digital assistants and digital cash cards come to mind. The lesson to be learned is that it is more important than ever to understand your customers and their needs.

THE CHALLENGE

By now you may have guessed where this is leading: your customers are increasingly embattled and bewildered by escalating demands, and they are passing these pressures on to you. The old ways of selling and doing business just won't cut it anymore.

Raising the Bar

As the bar is being raised for your customers, they are in turn raising it for you as a sales professional. Like billiard balls transferring their momentum to the other balls on the table, they will pass their escalating demands on to you and your competitors. And your competitors, responding to those same pressures, are getting better all the time. The bottom line for the sales professional: the habits, actions, and practices you followed in the past will not necessarily be enough. You cannot expect to enjoy the same level of success you have had in the past by doing the same things. *You must continually become better at what you do.*

Companies are demanding more and more of their suppliers. The pressure from the marketplace and their customers is passed on to you. They are demanding better service, higher quality, faster response, and lower prices. Your marketplace offers daunting challenges, but these are balanced by magnificent opportunities.

Reduction of Suppliers

Fortunately the relationship is not entirely one-sided. As the environment becomes more challenging, many firms are realizing that their best chances for survival rest on developing cooperative communities of mutual interest. These companies are forging new partnerships with suppliers, promising closer relationships and long-term contracts in exchange for greater demands. They have come to realize that it does not make sense to invest the time and effort to dig through mountains of information and find minute differences between a large selection of highly qualified suppliers every year when the contract comes up for renewal. Far better to spend that energy creating close relationships and real partnerships.

In return for granting longer-term contracts, the customer receives lower transaction costs, steeper learning curves, and preferential pricing, and finds that it is less expensive to manage the relationship over the long term. For example, Chrysler Corporation has slashed the number of suppliers it uses from 2,500 to 300. How would you like to be one of the 2,200 who has been shut out?

The result of the trend to partnerships is simple: it elevates the consequence of success or failure in the sales effort. The winners enjoy the stability of the long-term contract; the losers must wait that much longer to get another chance at the business, if it comes at all.

The new long-term relationships demand far more than mere price-performance comparisons, although they are still critical. If you would forge a true partnership with your customer, you must be able to create value in ways that your competitors can't, or your customers can't do for themselves.

Disintermediation

In *The Digital Economy*, Don Tapscott says, "Middleman functions between producers and consumers are being eliminated through digital networks."[1] As a salesperson, you are in effect a go-between connecting your company's production arm to the customer. The true function of an intermediary is to provide information and

1. Don Tapscott, *The Digital Economy*, McGraw-Hill, 1996, p. 56.

lower transaction costs. As information becomes more widely available, and direct communication becomes easier through the Internet and other technologies, intermediaries are needed less and less.

Your customers are "information affluent," with access to a tremendous amount of information about your products and those of your competitors. They have less of a need for you and the information you can provide. Following the simple laws of supply and demand, the more information that is available, the less valuable it is. In fact, the last thing your customers want is more information. They are already drowning in it. And if they do want it, they can usually get it through literature or the Internet. If you are to retain your value to your customer and your own firm, you must find ways to be more than just an intermediary. *You* must add value to the equation.

THE RESPONSE

So, how do you avoid being squeezed out? You must increase the value of the information you offer to customers, by turning it into knowledge and understanding. As information becomes worth less, knowledge becomes worth more.

My definition of knowledge is that it is *information put to good use.* In the confusing flood of information, the person who can bring a broad perspective, weaving together data and information from widespread sources to focus on and solve particular business problems, will become more and more valuable. Your customers do not have enough time to do this for every business problem they face. They will come to rely increasingly on those with this unique skill.

Knowledge is not just something that is already "there," ready to be plucked from a book or a computer screen by anybody who comes along. It is being created every day. Every time two or more pieces of information are brought together to provide a fresh perspective on an existing problem, knowledge is created. If this new idea results in a new way of doing things that helps a customer solve a problem or gives a customer the ability to accomplish what was previously out of reach, you have created value. The value is not there until somebody thinks of it. Yesterday's wealth resided in objects, but in today's world the principal source of most value is the creation of knowledge.

When you talk about adding value to your customers, what you are really doing is adding knowledge. You add value by creating knowledge about how to improve the customer's business. Knowledge creation results from the coming together of two major ingredients: intimate knowledge of your customer and expert knowledge of the application of your product or service.

Knowledge of customers means knowing a tremendous amount about how they add value to their customers, how they gain advantage over their competitors, the key drivers and measures of success in their industry, and their business processes. It means seeing the world through their eyes but seeing it in some ways better than they can.

Obviously you will not be an expert in all facets of a customer's business, or have solutions for all the company's problems. If you did, you might as well run the company. But what is possible is understanding a specific aspect of your customers' business operations better than they do, because that's what you specialize in, and as a professional you know more about that class of problems and opportunities than anyone else.

When you achieve this level of knowledge, you have the tools to set yourself apart from the competition. In a marketplace in which everybody is pushing the same thing, your differentiation and your edge will come only from fresh approaches to existing problems.

A Fish Story

To the novice, fishing looks pretty simple. Dip a hook into the water, and either a fish comes along and takes the bait, or it does not. There's not much more than luck involved.

People who know a little about fishing know it's a little more complicated than that. You need the right kind of gear, including rods and reels, the correct weight of line, and of course a complete selection of lures and baits. You also must know how to cast the lure where you want it to go, how to sense when a fish is nibbling, just the right time to set the hook, and how to play the fish so that you don't lose it once it is hooked. They know that skill at fishing does not come cheaply or quickly; there is much more than luck involved, although luck is still very important.

Those who know a lot about fishing, however, know that there is much more to it than just having the right equipment and knowing how to wield it skillfully, if you wish to be consistently successful. They know that beginner's luck sometimes happens, and sometimes even the best get skunked, but that only an elite few consistently find more fish than everybody else. Only an elite few can go out in the morning with the express intention of catching a particular kind of fish, not just anything that comes along, and come back in the afternoon more often than not having completed their mission. These elite fishermen are well respected by their peers, and many of them make a successful living at fishing, either as guides or as anglers themselves.

What makes the elite fishermen different from the rest of us is that they have a complete body of knowledge about the most important element in the fishing equation: the fish. They know what fish like to eat, where they like to go at different times, when they are likely to be biting. They can spot clues that are invisible to most of us but that tell them very clearly if a particular type of fish is in the area.

This range of skill applies equally to salespeople. There are a few who are like the complete novices; they may have a decent product at a reasonable price and be able to succeed for a short period of time, at least until the competitor introduces a better product. Most, however, are in the second category. They have a decent product and work hard at their selling skills, learning how to make presentations, handle objections, cold call successfully, and so on.

For you to be among the elite of sales professionals, the right equipment and skills are essential but not enough in themselves. Customer knowledge is also critical. Of course, you don't take your customers home and mount them on the wall, so that's where the analogy falls apart!

THE PAYOFF

The new sales challenge will create its own winners and losers. The winners will be those who make the changes necessary to adapt, while those who refuse to change will be left behind. If all of this sounds like hard work, it's because it is. That's why the payoff is so great.

The more difficult it is to master, the more valuable will be the elite few who do. You will be a member of a privileged minority. You see a few of them in almost every organization. Their sales seem effortless, because customers are usually calling them. They move easily through the corridors of corporate power. High-level executives take their calls, lower-level influencers call them for information. Their value to the organization matches the Pareto principle, by which the top 20 percent bring in 80 percent of the profits. They are usually well known in the industry, so even if they leave the company, they can easily find work in another organization and pick up with their clients with barely a wobble in the relationship.

Salespeople who can truly understand their customers and consistently help them improve their business processes are still so rare that their customers welcome them, and prospects seek them out. A recent study by the National Association of Purchasing Management revealed that 72 percent of buyers rated salespeople's knowledge of their businesses as low or very low. As one respondent said, "Frankly, salespeople don't have enough information to have intelligent conversations about their customers' businesses."[2]

When you approach the relationship as a partner, your expertise will give you the confidence and ability to gain access to senior-level executives in your prospect and customer organizations and, more important, to know what to say when you get there, so that you will be invited back. While you receive the personal gratification that comes from this, the real payoff is shorter sales cycles and long-term sales partnerships. Higher-level executives can make decisions faster, because the decision-making process does not have to work its way up to them, and they can make money available in the budget where none exists.

Shorter sales cycles are possible because jointly assigning a cost to the existing situation will create a sense of urgency for the decision. Many investment opportunities clamor for attention and budget, but those with real dollars attached to them speak louder and more clearly.

The complexity of many customer solutions today increasingly demands that you and your company team up with other vendors to deliver a complete system. In such a case, the team member who understands the customer best will be in a position to control the customer interface and command the highest profit margins. Addi-

---

2. Reported in *Sales and Marketing Management*, August 1996, p. 53.

tionally, future opportunities with that client will be much more likely to include you as the team's "most valuable player."

When your expertise is prized by your customers, price objections tend to diminish. Certainly your customers will not roll over and play dead for you, but if you have been imaginative enough to create real value for them, you will have done something your competitors have not, and that is value that is worth paying for.

Consistently understanding and fulfilling your customers' needs will help you retain customers longer. As a salesperson, you know how hard it can be to acquire new customers, so it makes sense to hold on to those you have. There are other payoffs for you and your company as well. Studies have shown that longer-term customers generally buy in larger amounts, are less focused on price, bring in new customers, and take less time in the sales cycle for each individual sales opportunity. In fact, these factors mean that reducing customer defections by as little as five percentage points can double profits.[3]

Probably the greatest benefit of selling in this way is that it gives you the power to frame the discussion and create the initiative within an account. Sun Tzu, whose classic *The Art of War* shaped the thinking of countless business leaders, said: "Knowledge of the problem is the key to the solution." If you can credibly understand your customers' business operations, you can help to define the problems. Often the solution is contained in the way the problem is defined, and if you can bring enough knowledge of your customers' business issues to bear, you can help define the problems that confront them. Be the first to define the problems and present the solutions, and your competitors will be playing catch-up.

OUTSIDE-IN THINKING

As management consultant Kenichi Ohmae aptly put it, ". . . strategy takes shape in the determination to create value for customers."[4]

3. "Learning from Customer Defections," Frederick Reichheld, *Harvard Business Review*, March–April 1996, p. 57.
4. "Getting Back to Strategy," Kenichi Ohmae, *Harvard Business Review*, November–December 1988, compiled in *Strategy*, Cynthia A. Montgomery and Michael E. Porter, eds., 1991.

Partnering requires a different mind-set from that of selling. Most salespeople look at their customers from the inside out; that is, their view of the sales process begins with themselves. They start with their own needs (to sell something and make money), their products, and the reputation of their company, and then go about looking for a place to fit them. They build their strategies around persuading their customers that their products are better than their competitors'.

As long as you are trying to do something *to* customers, this kind of thinking is probably enough. But if you intend to start doing things *with* customers, you must change your perspective.

To be truly successful in winning and keeping customer partnerships, you must start from the outside-in. It's a subtle but powerful shift in mind-set that looks at the sales process from the point of view of the customer first. What are the customer's needs? What keeps him awake at night and is the first thing he thinks about when he gets to work in the morning? What drives and excites your customer?

Your customers are not buyers who go to work in the morning thinking about what they plan to buy that day, or how they are going to spend their company's money. They are people who think about what they want to accomplish, the business and personal problems they face, and the opportunities of which they want to take advantage. Your only hope to forge a true partnership with these people is to first see the world through their eyes, and only then look inward to see what you bring to the table to make their lives easier. Remember, when you go fishing, it's not important which bait looks most appetizing to you.

Customers are your most important asset. Although you won't find them listed on your company's balance sheet, customers are truly your most important asset. They are the reason your company exists and the reason you have a job. These are the people who put food on your table. So, how much do you know about them?

HOW THIS BOOK CAN HELP YOU

The ability to create knowledge for your customers is built on a firm foundation of theoretical and practical business knowledge. This book will show you how to organize your search for information, and where to get it. Starting very generally, it gradually focuses down to specific business operations: how to understand them, improve them, and express the value of your improvements in the measurements your customers consider important. The "Action Points" at the end of each chapter will enable you to turn the concepts to practical use immediately.

Note

Because it is increasingly difficult today to separate products from services, the word "product" is used here to refer both to products and services, except where a distinction must be made. Also, the term "customer" refers to existing customers, potential customers, or prospects.

2

Creating Value

As we saw in Chapter 1, everyone, from purchasing departments to line business managers to top executives, is demanding greater value from suppliers. They want both the value your company brings and the value you deliver personally. If you aren't adding value, you and your company won't last over the long term. The short term doesn't look too bright, either.

To salespeople, this situation poses both a danger and an opportunity. If your product is not the lowest priced on the market, the danger to you as a salesperson is that your customers may define value too narrowly. They will define value as a product that meets the needs *they* also define, at the lowest possible price. Playing in this game quickly reduces your product to a commodity; as long as it meets minimum standards *as defined by the customer*, it will be judged solely on price. This type of selling is almost entirely reactive, and the main determinant of your success is efficiency in seeking out enough prospects so that you win your fair share of business. In this type of selling, to paraphrase Woody Allen: "Ninety percent of selling is just showing up." At this point your job is not really selling at all. It is order taking. Or, if there is any selling involved, it is usually the sales job you put on your manager to get the price the customer demands.

From a quality-of-life standpoint, this type of selling is just not that much fun, and it's not professionally rewarding. As we saw in the last chapter, it is also on its way out. As the information easily available to your customers grows, there is simply less and less reason to spend time with a live salesperson.

Of course, the very fact that you are reading this is pretty good evidence that you are way above the commodity stage. The question is, is there room for improvement in the value you can personally bring to your customers? To answer this question, this chapter will discuss two concepts: levels of value and elements of value. But first, it is important to establish how critical the role of perception is in your customers' decisions.

THE PERCEPTION OF VALUE

As you work your way through this book, you will become acquainted with a variety of tools and techniques for understanding the needs of your customers, making connections between your product and measurable business improvements, and expressing the value of your solution in financial language. However, you must keep in mind that all these tools are based on a central "fact of life" in sales: *the ultimate determinant of your success with any customer is that customer's perception of the value you bring.*

No matter how sure you are about the value you provide, or how many spreadsheets you complete, the value of your product is *zero* until the *customer* perceives a higher value. That perception of value will rest on objective and subjective factors. Logic and emotion both play a part.

Ultimately perception of value rests on objective factors. If your product does not deliver real value to the customer in the form of perceived business improvements, no amount of "smoke and mirrors" will keep you in that account for long. On the other hand, just having a better mousetrap does not guarantee a long line of folks at your door wanting to give you money. For one thing, the customer usually lacks important information to help him or her make the right decision, such as what your product does, how it works, and how it can be applied to the particular business situation to help the customer make more money. Even when customers do have a clear idea of how to apply the product for business advantage, their projections of expected benefit remain just that—projections—subject to unforeseen circumstances and unintended consequences.

There is also an important element of subjectivity involved. Every purchasing decision is ultimately based on a prediction of the future.

Predictions carry an element of risk, especially when money and business reputations are at stake. When there is risk involved, decisions and action are subject to the individual decision maker's perception of risk (which you can partially control) and personal tolerance for it.

As this discussion implies, you have the ability to influence your customer's perception of value, through both objective and subjective factors. Since you are the one asking for money, it is *your* responsibility, not the customer's, to create the perception of value.

Meeting the challenge of creating value in your customer's mind rests on the depth of knowledge you have about that customer. Because their purchasing decisions are based on subjective factors, your customers will assign different weights and values to different features of your product. So, the more you know about what is important to them, and the challenges and opportunities they face, the greater will be your chances of finding the right mix of features and arguments to create the highest perception of value in their minds.

LEVELS OF VALUE

The amount of value you bring to your customers will determine how they perceive you. In ascending order, the four levels of value are: commodity, feature-advantage-benefit, solution, and consultative. Let's take a look at each.

Commodity

"Tell me what you want, and I will get it for you at the lowest possible price."

At this level the customer sees no difference between your product and your competitors' offerings, including the value that you bring as a salesperson to the sale. In the customer's mind the only competitive differentiator is price. A product does not have to be simple or cheap to be perceived as a commodity. For example, this chapter is being typed on a notebook computer obtained through mail order. I did not see the computer or speak to a salesperson before purchasing it.

Although some products are perceived as commodities for objective reasons, frequently the principal contributor to this perception is the person trying to sell it. Many products that appear to be commodities on the surface can be distinguished in quite surprising ways when you make the effort to better define the product by looking at the entire range of benefits you bring the customer, not only via the product itself but also through the entire purchase and usage experience. Chapter 8, "Defining Your Product," will show you how to do this.

To succeed in the commodity space, the salesperson does not need to know anything about the customer, or even much about how the product will be used. To the customer, the value of the individual salesperson is virtually zero. The function of the salesperson could often be fulfilled as well or better by a catalog, a computer screen, or the customers themselves (as in self-serve machines). The principal value the salesperson brings is to make the product conveniently available to the customer when it is needed. If you are selling this way, the good news is that the customer does not expect much from you; the bad news is that you may soon be replaced by a catalog or a website.

Feature-Advantage-Benefit (FAB) Vendor

"Tell me your requirements, and I will tell you the best alternative."

In this case the salesperson is able to point out differences between his or her product and the competitors'. The salesperson knows the product's features very well, how they compare with the competition, and the benefit those features bring to the customer. He or she can point out distinguishing characteristics that make this product better than the competitors' and what each of them means to the person buying it. To accomplish this successfully, the salesperson must know what the product does and how it is used. This means knowing a little about the customer's business operations, enough to distinguish between competing alternatives and recommend the best choice for that situation.

At the FAB level, the salesperson is adding some value to the customer. The principal value lies in the time and effort the buyer does not have to expend, because the salesperson brings knowledge about specific products that the customer does not have. At the same time, the salesperson can help reduce risk in the decision by providing valuable information about the consequences of specific choices. The customer expects that the technical salesperson will have a strong knowledge of the product and competitors' products.

FAB vendors are still in a reactive mode, because their customers know what they want and understand their own requirements.

Solution

"Tell me how you want to do things, and I will help you put together the best way to do it."

The FAB vendor progresses to the solution-seller level by acquiring two habits. First, instead of beginning with the product and relating it to customer benefits, the solution seller leads off with the needs of the buyer. Additionally, the salesperson sees the product as a total package rather than a collection of features and is therefore better able to relate the use of the product to solve problems posed by customers. He or she knows how the product fits into a system of products and components which can work together to solve the customer's operational challenges. The solution-oriented sales professional is still reactive to a certain extent, because the customers generally have specified their own business needs and translated them into system requirements.

Solution sellers may also be able to express the value of their solutions in financial measurements such as return on investment and net present value. However, the principal expression of value is in operational terms: how the product can help the customer shave time off a cycle for example, or increase the yield from a manufacturing process. To succeed, the salesperson must know a lot about the customer's business operations and processes, although much of that knowledge may derive more from understanding the horizontal or vertical process than from the customer's specific business goals. For example, you may know a lot about applying your software to improve a manufacturing process, and be able to turn that knowledge into valuable solutions for your customer, without needing to know much about the customer's broader business goals and strategies.

The customer's expectations are quite high at the solution level. Customers expect the salesperson to thoroughly understand the product, how it interacts with other necessary components, and the effect it has on business operations. They may also expect some help in cost-justifying the purchase decision.

Consultative

"Tell me where you want to go, and I will show you the best way to get there."

This level is the pinnacle of skill of the sales professional. At the consultative level, the sales professional understands the customer's business goals and strategies and is able to point out ways to help the customer achieve those goals. Here you are able to move beyond simply reacting to customers' expressed needs and can help them realize that they have needs they were not aware of.

This level of selling requires a tremendous amount of customer knowledge and enough business and industry knowledge to place that information in the proper context. The perceived level of value brought by the salesperson is extremely high, because such people are able to make a real difference in the way the customer does business. They become strategic partners, which means that they are a trusted resource who may often be brought in on the customer's plans at an early stage. They may shape their customer's plans instead of merely jumping when the customer announces them.

The customer's expectations from the consultative sales professional are even higher than at the solution level. If you want to play in this space, you must have more than operational knowledge or skill; you must also be able to relate the processes in which you specialize to the customer's business goals and connect the consequences of business improvements to lasting business improvements for your customer. However, the payoffs can also be tremendous.

Although the initial sale may take longer at the consultative level, subsequent sales to that customer can happen much faster. Showing that you understand the customer's business and are a valuable resource for business improvements moves you from the transaction space to the relationship space. At the lower levels, no matter how successful you are with each sales opportunity, every new deal that comes up is a separate transaction, where you must prove yourself all over again. When you have established yourself as a trusted business partner, you will have the inside track on any new opportunities, and the business is yours to lose. You have earned that right, and you have established the connections and relationships at higher levels within the customer's organization. This will make it much more likely that you will be involved at an early stage in helping to shape the company's plans.

THE PROFIT WEDGE

To climb the levels of value, we need to fully understand the elements of value that we can deliver to our customer. As introduction, let us first take a look at this concept called the profit wedge.

In the training seminars I run, I often hear from salespeople that their product is only a commodity. They say they would like to be consultative sellers, but the product they sell prevents them. Their competitor's product is just as good, the customer sees very little if any difference between competing alternatives, and the only way to compete is to provide the lowest price.

There is definitely a lot of truth to these claims, but often it is a self-fulfilling prophecy. If you think that there is very little difference between what you have to offer and your competitor's product, then how can you expect that your customers will think any differently? In sales, the first person you have to convince is yourself.

Fortunately there is a way out of this conundrum. While it is unrealistic to think that buyers will ever stop looking for the best deal for themselves, it is up to you to change the rules of the game to make them more in your favor. The trick is to get out of the product space and concentrate on the effect you have on your customer's business. Take a look at Figure 2-1.

The top line represents your customer's total revenues. In a normal economy, that line trends very slowly upward over time. The average sales growth of Fortune 500 companies (adjusted for inflation and not counting mergers and acquisitions) may be less than 2 percent per

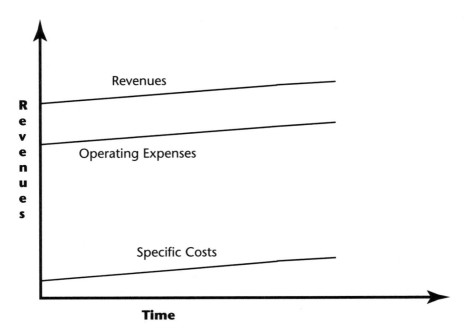

Figure 2-1.   Revenues Versus Expenses over Time

year.[1] From your customer's point of view, the bad news is that total operating expenses (the second line) usually keep pace with the revenue trend. This means that profits grow very slowly, if at all.

Now look at the lowest line on the graph—specific costs. This represents the portion of your customer's expenses devoted to the product category you sell. In many cases, if the line were drawn to scale, it would not even show up on the graph.

The mistake that most salespeople make is that they focus all their attention on that lowest line. Now, suppose that you are able to come to your customers with a significantly lower price for your product. You're in good shape, right? Let's see how that result looks on the graph.

1. Between 1983 and 1993, the rate of growth for Fortune 500 industrial companies was −0.33 percent (adjusted for inflation) and for Fortune 500 companies, 2.2 percent, as reported in *Grow to Be Great*, by Dwight L. Gertz and Joao Baptista, Free Press, 1995, p. 22.

Best case, it looks like Figure 2-2. Not too bad, when you look at it from a narrow point of view; but stop and think what that graph means to you from a long-term, strategic-partner point of view. Even if you could produce the results shown here, how significant is your benefit in relation to your customer's main problem, which is to increase profits? How much attention do you suppose you will be able to get from the customer's higher-level executives? What if the customer has higher priorities for spending money?

If the answers to these questions made you feel a little uncomfortable, look at the graph in Figure 2-3.

Figure 2-3 simply says that the best way to add value to your customers, the kind of value that makes a real difference and is noticed at high levels, is to use your product or service to drive a "wedge" between their revenues and operating expenses. Combining the attributes of your product, your knowledge of the customer's business operations, and your imagination, you will be able to demonstrate how your product will help your customers increase their

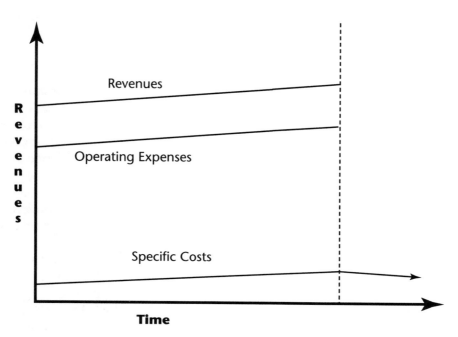

Figure 2-2.   Decreasing Specific Costs Makes Little Difference

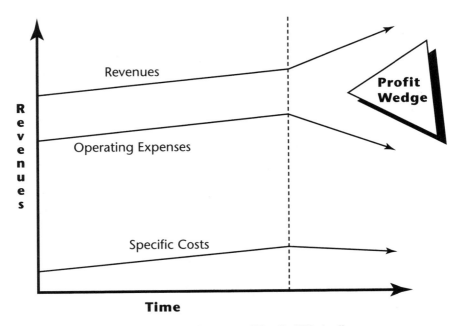

Figure 2-3. Impact of Profit "Wedge"

revenues, decrease their operating expenses, or some combination of both.

If you are able to do this, the total value added to your customer can be far in excess of the expense involved in purchasing your product. In fact, knowing how to do this will give you the confidence to tell your customers that you are not there to reduce their costs related to your product: after buying from you *they may actually spend more but be better off for it.* Too many purchasing managers—and too many salespeople—think that purchasing is about spending less. It's not. It is about making more.

Another mistake that many salespeople make is to assume that customers always know what is good for them; that they will know exactly how to get maximum benefit out of the products they purchase or know exactly what they will get when they do. Nothing could be further from the truth. It is not the customers' job to figure out the value they will get from your product; it is your job.

Playing in the profit wedge space is a way to change the rules of the game and tilt them in your favor. If competitors offer a comparable product at a lower price, you can bet that they will try to frame the discussion so that it never leaves the lowest line in the graph. Using the profit wedge approach will help you to:

- Increase the perceived value of your product.
- Reduce the emphasis on price as a factor in the decision.
- Increase the customer's sense of urgency to implement your solution.
- Open doors for you at higher levels within the customer's organization.
- Establish yourself as a resource to help the customer with business issues.
- Differentiate yourself from your competitors.

If the benefits of profit wedge selling are so obvious, why isn't everybody doing it? The answer is simple: it's hard work. To be able to play in this space, you need skills that supplement your basic selling skills and product knowledge. As you can see, in this type of selling, it's not product knowledge that is important; it's customer knowledge. You must know enough about your customer's business operations to credibly make the connection between your product and measurable business impact. You must also know enough about business and financial concepts and terminology to speak the language of high-level decision makers. When you have these skills, you can see that the profit wedge concept affords you several ways you can bring value to your customers. The value does not rest in your product; it rests in your ability to relate the application of your product to improvements in your customer's business.

ELEMENTS OF VALUE

Climbing the partnership pyramid and playing in the profit wedge space requires you to consistently present a full range of value to your customers.

The first two elements of value are fairly basic: price and cost. Price is pretty simple. It is the amount of money your customer pays to purchase your product. It is primarily the invoice cost of the product, but it can also comprise less obvious expenses such as transaction costs and any related expenses required to get the product installed and working as it should.

Cost is a slightly more difficult element to measure, because it transcends simple invoice cost. Many products do not come right out of a box and begin working immediately for the customer. There might be a lot of work or expenditure necessary on the customer's part to get the product to deliver the expected value. If a lower-priced component requires some rework to make it fit or to meet the necessary standards, is it really lower cost? Or what about a product that costs less up front but breaks down more often? As you can see, the entire concept of cost, or *total cost of ownership* (TCO), can be a critical issue in determining the value you bring to your customer. We will revisit this concept in more detail in Chapter 9.

Price and cost are the most basic elements of the value you bring. At the next level, you must be able to relate the use or application of your product to the improvement of business performance. There are literally thousands of business activities and processes that might be changed or improved in some way, and the performance improvement will show up in one or more of three dimensions.

To provide a general framework for understanding the dimensions of business performance, let's consider the standard productivity equation:

$$\text{Productivity} = \frac{\text{Output}}{\text{Input}}$$

This equation may seem to say it all, but the increasing competitiveness of global business and accelerating technological change have joined together to add a third dimension to the focus on performance:

$$\text{Productivity} = \frac{\text{Output}}{\text{Input}} \times \text{Speed}$$

Using this formula as a framework, you can see the next three elements of value: use your product to increase some measure of your customer's output, reduce the inputs required, and help the customer to do the entire process faster. In the language of *Bottom-Line Selling* these three elements are effectiveness, efficiency, and speed.

Effectiveness concentrates on the "top line" of the customer's income statement. It correlates to revenue growth, quality, and customer satisfaction. As the current business pendulum swings from downsizing to growth, it is becoming more and more important in the minds of your customers. Effectiveness improvements can be a tougher concept to deal with than simply cutting costs. It is much easier to look at a process and spot what should be removed than to imagine what should be added. Improvements in effectiveness require intimate knowledge of *how your customers add value to their customers.*

Efficiency correlates to reductions in the cost of the customer's business processes, through lower prices of inputs, reductions of inputs, elimination of steps, and so forth. This has long been the most common area on which salespeople and customers concentrate. One reason is that it is usually the first question our customers have, and it is especially pressing with the recent emphasis on downsizing. You can find efficiency improvements by intimately understanding your customers' processes.

Speed, the third leg, could logically be included within the first two, but it is fast becoming a critical competitive arena in its own right. Speed refers to reductions in the cycle required to serve customers. It includes the time from when a need is first discerned in the marketplace to when the company receives payment for fulfilling that need. As such, it includes new-product introduction, manufacturing, delivery, service, collections—in short, practically every facet of business today. A perfect example of the importance of cycle time in business today is the retail industry. An important factor in Wal-Mart's meteoric growth has been its ability to wring every unnecessary second out of the replenishment cycle.

These three areas of business improvement can complement or conflict with each other. For example, reductions in cycle time can reduce costs through reductions in inventory and increase effectiveness by introducing new products faster. On the other hand, improvements in effectiveness through better service may mean higher costs.

Thus far in the discussion, the elements of value are fairly easy to measure. But there is an even higher level which may be more difficult to measure but no less important. The highest level is the strategic fit, which is where you are able to show your customers how you can help them achieve their strategic business goals. These might include specific market-share targets, opening new markets, changing the way they do business, and other approaches which are covered in detail in Chapter 12. At this level the other elements are still extremely important, but the value you add consists of tying them all together in a strategic package: individual investment opportunities are seen as components in a longer-term strategic plan rather than as discrete events. The strategic fit also deals with helping your customer achieve gains in less measurable areas such as reducing business risk, improving the corporate image, keeping up with competitors, and attracting and motivating the best people.

SUMMARY

Before we proceed with the tools and techniques of bottom-line selling, let's pause and reflect on what must be done. We know that the responsibility for consistent sales success is in our hands. We have the ability—and the responsibility—to make the difference in our customer's perception of the value of our product. We do that through demonstrating the business impact of our solution, and this in turn requires an intimate understanding of the customer's business operations and challenges. To help you get to this level, this book takes you through three components. First, we will look at the tools and concepts to *understand* our customers' businesses, then learn all the ways that we can *fix or improve* their business processes, and finally pull it all together with the skills to *sell* our solution.

Part 2

Understanding

3

Reading Annual Reports

The best place to start our quest to understand our customer's business operations is the document they use to explain themselves to the world: their annual report. Every public company is required by the Securities and Exchange Commission to issue a report containing specified information to the public. While the principal audience is the company's stockholders, the report is also intended for use by suppliers, creditors, customers, employees, and assorted other stakeholders. As such, it is written under specific rules designed to answer the needs of the various constituencies, so it is not all things to all people. Probably nobody reading the annual report will find that it specifically meets his or her needs, but focused reading can yield significant information, especially for the salesperson. It is, quite simply, your principal document for getting to know a company.

The core of the annual report is the financial statements contained in them, but you would not know that from looking at one. The financial information is the drab numerical text usually buried near the back of the report (which most investors never read beyond a cursory glance), sandwiched between glossy pictures of company products, personnel, and customers as well as vision statements in the front and dignified photos of the board of directors in the back.

Although compliance with legal requirements is the original reason for issuing an annual report, businesses turn this necessary evil to their advantage by using it to showcase the company. Remember that the bulk of the annual report is written by the company's PR department. In fact, the annual report is often the premier piece of sales literature the company produces—designed to sell the company's most important product: its stock.

For selling purposes, you can usually glean as much from the written material in the annual report as you can from the financial information itself. This chapter concentrates on the supporting written portion, and the next chapter will take you on a guided tour through the numbers.

WHY SHOULD YOU READ THEM?

The typical corporate annual report does not make for exciting reading, but when read with a specific focus, it can be interesting and profitable. Here are some of the important reasons you should read them.

Consultative Selling

As we have seen, sales professionals in the complex selling environment succeed best when they can be perceived as consultants and partners to their customers. Enduring, mutually profitable partnerships can be formed only when the customer perceives that the salesperson adds value beyond the specific product offered. This is possible only through an intimate knowledge of the customer's business, sources of competitive advantage, strengths, weaknesses, challenges, and opportunities. One of the best sources of this information is the annual report.

Earning the Right

The knowledge about the company contained in the annual report is the minimum price of admission to meet with high-level executives.

Knowing the Score

If the goal of the consultative sales professional is to improve customers' business operations, the annual report is the scorecard that shows how effectively and efficiently those business operations are conducted. You need to read it to know the score.

Speaking the Language

The annual report will show you what management considers to be important, which internal and external business measurements they focus on, the buzzwords they use, and prevailing corporate practices and initiatives.

Seeing the Destination

Creating a true partnership with your customers means becoming a part of their planning process. You can help them plan to reach their destination if you know what the principal destination is: What is the company's vision, what does it intend to accomplish, what are its specific business strategies, and what is the timetable?

OBTAINING AN ANNUAL REPORT

The easiest way to obtain an annual report for a publicly owned company is to simply call the company and ask for one. Call the main headquarters number and tell the receptionist you would like a copy of the annual report. The investor relations department will take your name and address and send one to you within several days. Although some companies say they send them only to shareholders, they rarely ask and even more rarely refuse if you are not a shareholder.

BEFORE YOU PLUNGE IN

In working with your customers' annual reports, keep two important points in mind. The first should go without saying, but my experience in training salespeople over the years leads me to say it anyway: *just read it.* Many salespeople "check a box" in their sales cycle by obtaining their customer's annual report but often fail to give it more than a cursory review. Read it in detail at least twice. This advice can do more for you than the rest of this book. Second, read purposefully; have a goal in mind when reading it. Looking for specific things will make the material more meaningful.

ANNUAL REPORT COMPONENTS

There's a lot of "fluff" in the annual report, but don't dismiss it. This is where you will find most of your useful sales information. Figure 3-1

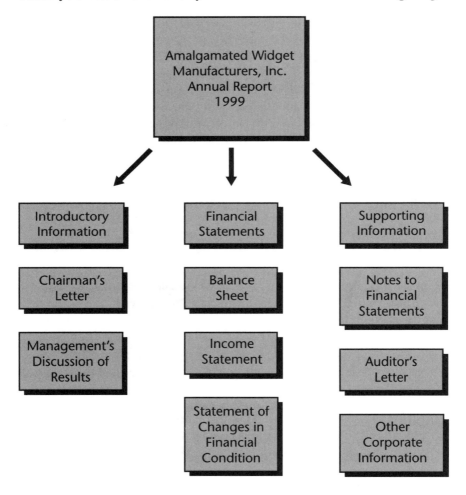

Figure 3-1. Principal Parts of the Annual Report

shows the principal parts that you will find in every annual report, but don't be concerned if the one you have varies slightly. There will often be other sections added to aid the company in getting across the message it wishes to communicate, and some of the sections will be there but in a different name. While these sections are required by law, there is ample room for individual company creativity where the law does not dictate.

How to Read the Introductory Section

The introductory section of the annual report is usually the longest. You will notice that it contains a lot of promotional information, including flattering pictures of the company and its employees, products, and sometimes customers. Usually the tone is upbeat and optimistic. Sometimes this section can be as noteworthy for what it leaves out as for what it includes, and it takes a close reading between the lines to figure out what is being said.

Chairman's Letter to Shareholders

In the chairman's letter, the chairman of the board of directors sends a message about the state of the company. Its primary purpose is to tout the company as an investment to shareholders, so this section can be pretty vague or even misleading, especially if there is not that much good news to report. While this can make it tough on potential investors who are trying to get an accurate picture of the state of the company, it can be very useful to a salesperson trying to find out what the company considers important and what management is concerned or excited about. The trick to getting anything out of reading one is to have a specific focus.

The principal focus for a salesperson reading an annual report is to discover:

- Hard evidence of a need for your product or service (potential problems you might be able to solve)
- At least a plausible reason why a high-level executive in that company might want to see you

- What the company does and how it does it
- Language you can use in your sales approach

The Top 10 Things to Look For

Keep the following questions in mind as you read the chairman's letter and other introductory information in the report. Although your customer's annual report may not contain complete answers, asking the questions will help to focus your reading. This will make your reading more productive and will suggest many other excellent questions to ask your customer. This is the basic information you should know. In Chapter 6 we will learn to use other easily accessible sources to fill in the gaps left by the annual report as well as to double-check the accuracy of information.

1. What is the company's vision or mission statement?

Take a moment to read Ameritech's vision statement from its 1997 annual report:

> Ameritech will be the world's premier provider of full-service communications for people at work, at home or on the move. Our goal is to improve the quality of life for individuals and to increase the competitive effectiveness of the businesses we serve. As we move and manage information for our customers, we set standards for value and quality. Ameritech's competence reaches worldwide, building on our strength in America's vibrant upper Midwest. Customers can be assured that we will assume only those tasks we can do exceedingly well.

Ameritech obviously put a lot of time, thought, and money into crafting that vision statement. The important questions are Why? and How can a salesperson use it to advantage?

Vision statements have been much in vogue in the past several years, and it's tempting to cynically dismiss them as being fluff dreamed up by the public relations department. However, in this age of flatter organizations and employee empowerment, vision statements can serve to galvanize and guide the efforts of thousands of employees in a common direction. Many companies (though not all) use their vision statements as general frameworks for their specific business strategies and investment decisions. According to the authors of *Vision in Action*:

> . . . vision or strategy is about what an organization wants to be in terms of products, markets, and resources or capabilities. In today's uncertain and extremely competitive business environment, continued success depends as much on the quality of strategic thinking—and on how well that thinking becomes imprinted on every decision an organization makes—as it does on the effectiveness of operations.[1]

While your customer's corporate culture will dictate how seriously the vision is taken as a guide to action, the vision statement often affects decisions that are made. This includes purchasing decisions.

Of course, most of the executives with whom you will be dealing have their own personal or business visions, which are aligned with the corporate vision. Knowing the vision statement can help you earn the right to explore their personal visions. It can also help place the investment decision for your product within the accepted framework.

2. What are the principal strategies in place to reach that vision?

The bridges between the company's vision and eventual reality are the strategies being followed to achieve it. Strategies reflect the economic realities of the business environment and describe how the company will deploy its resources for competitive advantage. Typically a company will list three to five specific business strategies. Knowing the strategies will help you draw the connection between your product and the achievement of a specific company goal. Here's an example from Microsoft's 1997 annual report:

> Reduce the Total Cost of Ownership and improve manageability.
> Reduce complexity.
> Focus on handheld devices.
> Exploit the integration of PC and TV technology.

1. Benjamin B. Tregoe, John W. Zimmerman, Ronald A. Smith, and Peter M. Tobia, *Vision in Action*, Simon and Schuster, 1989, p. 12.

As you review your customer's strategies, keep the following questions in mind:

- Do they have a target date for achievement?
- How will they measure success?
- Who is responsible for each strategy?
- What specific projects and investments will be made to support each strategy?

3. What are the principal lines of business, and where are they?

Many public companies are so large that they are truly several enterprises rolled into one. Often the value your product adds is more appropriate at the individual line-of-business level or in specific geographic locations. The more you know about the various businesses the company is in, the more opportunities for selling your product may be found. Pay particular attention to recent acquisitions, which can be clues about the direction the company is pursuing and can be new markets for you within that company.

4. Who are the customers?

Companies love to talk in their annual reports about the ways they are helping their customers. These examples can help you understand how they add value to their customers. In a very important sense, you are selling competitive advantage to your customers. This means being able to add more value, at a lower price, to the customers they serve. The more you know about their customers, the easier it is to make the connection. You also may be able to use their examples as analogies to illustrate ways in which you can help them.

You should also understand the markets your customer is in—and intends to be in. As an example, Hewlett-Packard discusses in its 1997 annual report its aggressive emphasis on sales to the small-business market, noting its ". . . products, services and programs for these customers, who make up the fastest-growing part of the business market."

5. What significant challenges does the company face in achieving its vision?

Every business faces significant challenges in fulfilling its vision, executing its strategies, or growing revenues and market share. These challenges typically come from current or future competition, industry or economic trends, market acceptance of products, and so forth. Frequently you will have to use critical reading skills to read between the lines, as many companies do not play up the dark clouds on the horizon (because of the effect on the stock price).

Knowing their challenges may help you anticipate needs and discuss similar challenges you have helped solve for other customers. Example:

> Due to changing consumer preferences, technology and deregulation, the traditional core deposit business is in long-term secular decline. Our challenge is to manage this decline and to increase the profitability of the total customer relationship even as core deposit profitability shrinks.
>
> *National City Corporation, 1997*

6. What significant events impacted performance during the previous year?

What happened during the year covered by the report that affects current strategies or decisions? What is the company proud of, or what is it struggling with? For example, in 1997 and 1998 many companies were impacted by the Asian financial crisis; some were affected by events specific to them, such as Office Depot's canceled merger plans with Staples.

Keep in mind that these significant events may be "old news." Because they are not reported until the end of the fiscal year, and there is a year between annual reports, the report you have could be more than a year out of date.

7. What key measurements does the company use to indicate success?

The common language of annual reports is the financial measurements on which Wall Street tends to focus: earnings, revenue growth, and earnings per share. You will find ample references to these measures in the annual reports you read.

However, most business managers use other measures to ensure that they are on track to their targets, and you need to know these too. These measures may be specific to their industry or the particular process they are responsible for. For example, a football team ultimately wins or loses based on the final score, but individual team members are evaluated and compensated based on other statistics, such as number of tackles, yards gained, or interceptions. Each sport has different measures, and each position within that sport is evaluated differently. It's the same with business.

Knowing these measurements will help you present the value of your solution in terms that are most meaningful to the individuals to whom you are selling. If you know how they are measured and compensated, you can adapt your presentation of the benefits in terms of the language that is most meaningful to them. You will also find that knowing these measures can significantly add to your personal credibility. This topic is so important that it is covered in full detail in its own chapter, "Making Sense of the Numbers" (Chapter 5), but here are two examples:

- General Electric spends three pages of its annual report discussing its pursuit of six-sigma quality in everything it does, and what that means to the company.
- Clorox uses a measure called the Clorox Value Measure, which relates asset use to profitability.

What specific performance measures does your customer use?

8. Who are the executives responsible for each of the principal strategies and business measurements?

As you begin to concentrate your business-improvement efforts on specific divisions or helping the customer execute individual strategies, you will inevitably be solving problems for the real people charged with those issues. These people are the problem owners who stand to benefit the most from the solution you can provide. They will become your key decision makers and inside salespeople because they have a real stake in the solution selected.

The annual report can help you target your initial efforts to contact a prospect or can help you widen the scope of your influence with existing customers.

The usual annual report might list the individuals responsible for specific formal divisions without detailing the individuals responsible for the results to be achieved. However, you will be able to at least get clues about where to begin your search.

9. Who are the company's major competitors, and how does it compare with them?

It is not often that the annual report will talk about the competition by name, but you may find clues about rivals and what the company has planned to win the competitive edge. You should keep in mind the following questions: Where does your customer rank in its industry? Who is the most important competitor? How does it compare with them?

In fact, to know your customer intimately, it helps to study competitors' annual reports. Later in this book you will learn to evaluate key performance measures of the specific industry you are targeting. The number you calculate for your customer is meaningless by itself. It has significance only when compared with the competition.

10. What are the principal sources of competitive advantage?

It's easy to get lost in all the discussion in the annual report and to get confused by all the detail. However, when you peel through all the fluff and the various layers of analysis, most businesses succeed or fail based on a very few simple factors. In some industries, it might be the ability to be the low-cost producer, or the skills to develop new products faster, or on-time delivery, or superior location.

If you are selling competitive advantage, you must know the critical success factors that will determine whether your customer will be able to deliver value to its customers at a competitive price. These factors vary by industry and may even vary by company within an industry. For example, in the airline industry, some carriers are successful by concentrating on operational efficiencies to deliver the lowest price to their customers, while others focus on delivering superior service at a higher price. In Chapter 7 we will explore the concept of the value chain, which is a useful framework for describing and evaluating a firm's sources of competitive advantage.

Management's Discussion of Results

Management's discussion will help you supplement the chairman's letter as a source of answers to the Top 10 questions. This section is required by the SEC, so it is not written by the public relations department. You will typically find more "hard" information about business operations which can be useful in understanding the issues the company faces. While this section is more objective, it still can be viewed, albeit cynically, as an attempt by management to put its spin on the operating results in the financial statements.

By law, management is required to report on results of operations, capital resources, and liquidity. The company must also discuss conditions and uncertainties that may materially affect the business. You will revisit this section in more detail later as you begin to examine the financial statements, especially the income statement, because management's discussion can be very helpful in explaining the reasons behind the numbers. Following are the categories of information found in this section.

Major Business and Financial Events Both in the Past and Anticipated for the Future

Business events are discussed in more objective language than in the chairman's letter, usually with explanations tying the events to the results shown on the financial statements you are about to read. For example, revenue increases (or declines) will usually be explained in terms of different product lines, price increases or volume growth, or geographical expansion. Often, when adding up all the revenue increases discussed, you will find that they total more than the total revenue growth. This can only mean that other areas not discussed had declines. That's a way to read between the lines to find areas where there could be room for improvement or concern on the part of the company. If it is your job to solve problems for your customers, that job sometimes means uncovering the problems that they will not readily acknowledge.

Acquisitions and Divestitures

When evaluating revenue growth or decline, you must be aware if any dramatic changes in revenue are the result of fundamental changes in business operations, or merely the result of new companies having been acquired or divested during the year. If the change is due to acquisition, it may suggest a possible new source of business for you within your existing customer. If the change is caused by alterations in the company's strategies, its execution of those strategies, or its markets, you can be sure these conditions will be uppermost in the minds of your customers, and you should be aware of them.

Business Strategies

The operating results are the best measure of progress toward achieving certain business strategies discussed earlier. Since individual businesses or strategies will not show up in the consolidated financial numbers, this section is often the only place to find information about specifics.

Explanation of Operating Results

The final numbers you read in the financial section are very general summaries of literally millions of transactions, decisions, and business processes that occurred during the year. The explanation of operating results will help you understand the main impacts on revenue growth. In a retail operation, was growth caused by opening new stores, or more productivity per store? Did its revenue grow more or less than its competitors'? How was revenue growth impacted by acquisitions or divestitures? Did growth come from shipping more units, charging higher prices, or some combination?

Details of Operating Results by Geographic Segment or Business Unit

Except when dealing with the most senior-level management, most of the individual buyers with whom you will work are concerned with their own particular patches. Management's discussion frequently provides the detail that is not discernible in the consolidated numbers.

Key Business or Financial Measurements

Many company-specific measurements can be found. These often have more meaning to your buyers than goals over which they have little control, such as earnings per share.

Supporting Information

On the back of the financial statements in the annual report you will find some other information that can also be useful.

Notes to Financial Statements

The notes provide further explanatory or clarifying information that goes behind the numbers of the financial statements. Written by the accounting firm that audited the financial statements, this section is by design very objective and complete in all material respects. Much of it is boilerplate, but it can sometimes supply important information not easily found in the introductory sections. For example, details about depreciation might be needed later in the sales cycle as you prepare a financial proposal to justify the return on investment for your product.

Corporate Information

In the back of the annual report you will find listings of principal corporate officers and the board of directors, sometimes with photographs, which can help you identify specific individuals to contact. Sometimes the composition of the board can work to your advantage or disadvantage, depending on whether your company or your competitor has influence there. Either way, it is helpful to know. There may even be times where you recognize an individual from his or her picture and can take advantage of a chance meeting in an elevator or in the halls. It happens more often than you might think.

ACTION POINTS

1. Get copies of the annual reports for your top customers and prospects.
2. Read them, keeping the Top 10 questions in mind. Keep paper and pen handy for taking notes, and start keeping your information in its own section in your customer file.

4

The Financial Statements

So far, we have not talked about the real meat of the annual report—the financial statements. While those rows of numbers may seem intimidating at first, if you keep in mind one basic rule we have already talked about you will emerge unscathed and a little bit the wiser for it: if you know what you are looking for, it is much easier to find, and you will waste little time with the trivial and the irrelevant.

This chapter covers the vocabulary you need to converse intelligently with higher-level decision makers and to make sense of the business concepts in subsequent chapters. One promise: this is not Accounting 101; we will spend most of our time on the parts of the financial statement with which you must be familiar to help you sell.

BASIC FINANCIAL STATEMENT STRUCTURE

This discussion will take you on a guided tour to familiarize you with the landscape of the financial statement section. The first thing you will notice is that the section is broken into three parts, as shown in Figure 4-1:

The **balance sheet** lists what the company owns and what it owes. It is a snapshot taken at a moment in time (the end of the company's fiscal year, in the case of the annual report).

The **income statement** reports the revenues earned by the company during the financial period (usually the previous year) minus the expenses required to earn those revenues. If the balance sheet is

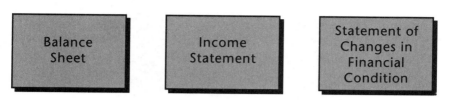

Figure 4-1.   Financial Statements Section

a snapshot, the income statement is a movie which shows the results of the company's operations during the entire year. This section contains the proverbial "bottom line."

The **statement of changes in financial condition** bridges the gap between the balance sheet and income statement by showing how the results of operations changed the balance sheet during the year. All of the changes are expressed in terms of cash. It answers the question: how much flowed into and out of the company during the year?

Let's dig into each section in a little more detail, focusing on the business functions that cause the numbers you see on the page. As you follow the description of the various categories shown on the financial statements, keep in mind one very important point: *the numbers are not reality.*

This simply means that the numbers shown on the financial statements are the results of estimates, opinions, accounting standards, and sometimes heated argument. They are close representations of the results of real business processes, decisions, and actions. Therefore it is important to understand the underlying business processes that result in the numbers shown. The financial statements tell you the "final score" of the game but do not describe the way the game was played.

THE BALANCE SHEET

The balance sheet is a listing of everything the company owns and everything it owes. Look at the actual balance sheet from the Rockwell International Corporation 1997 annual report as shown in Figure 4-2.

Consolidated Balance Sheet   Rockwell International Corporation
(in millions)

September 30		1997	1996
Assets	**Current assets**		
	Cash (includes time deposits and certificates of		
	deposit: 1997, $189 million; 1996, $411 million)	**$ 283**	$ 663
	Receivables	**1,319**	1,206
	Inventories	**1,526**	1,481
	Other current assets	**556**	496
	Net assets of Automotive Business	**—**	612
	Net assets of Graphic Systems	**—**	560
	Total current assets	**3,684**	5,018
	Property		
	Land	**88**	83
	Land and leasehold improvements	**70**	69
	Buildings	**768**	760
	Machinery and equipment	**2,020**	1,827
	Office and data processing equipment	**651**	563
	Construction in progress	**527**	380
	Total	**4,124**	3,682
	Less accumulated depreciation	**1,879**	1,674
	Net property	**2,245**	2,008
	Intangible assets	**1,789**	1,762
	Other assets	**253**	188
	Total	**$7,971**	$8,976
Liabilities and	**Current liabilities**		
Shareowners'	Short-term debt	**$ 66**	$ 323
Equity	Accounts payable—trade	**840**	801
	Accrued compensation and benefits	**436**	391
	Accrued income taxes	**96**	155
	Other current liabilities	**532**	565
	Net liabilities of A&D business	**—**	1,309
	Total current liabilities	**1,970**	3,544
	Long-term debt	**156**	156
	Accrued retirement benefits	**795**	764
	Other liabilities	**239**	256
	Shareowners' equity		
	Common stock (shares issued: 1997, 216.4		
	million; 1996, 209.5 million)	**216**	210
	Class A common stock (shares issued: 1996,		
	27.9 million)	**—**	28
	Additional paid-in capital	**901**	199
	Retained earnings	**4,409**	4,466
	Currency translation	**(103)**	(103)
	Common stock in treasury, at cost	**(612)**	(544)
	Total shareowners' equity	**4,811**	4,256
	Total	**$7,971**	$8,976

See notes to financial statements

Figure 4-2.   Balance Sheet

First, a few things to keep in mind:

- At the top, just near the company name, the accountants will specify the "scale" of the balance sheet. In this case every dollar shown on the balance sheet is equivalent to $1 million. So, the total assets shown are actually almost $8 billion. ("Consolidated" as used in financial statements simply means that all of the various divisions have been consolidated into one statement.)
- Notice the dates. Every balance sheet will show at least the most current two years, with the most current year shown first. In this case the date is September 30, 1997.
- Think of the balance sheet as a snapshot taken at the close of business at the end of the company's fiscal year. (Never call it a physical year. You will sound funny.) In reality, these accounts may change hundreds if not thousands of times a day as various transactions affect the balances. The picture you see is frozen at a particular moment in time.
- At the top half of the balance sheet are listed the **assets**, which are simply resources owned or controlled by the company which can be used to earn a profit. On the bottom half are listed **liabilities** and **shareowners' equity**, which are debts owed to outside creditors and to the owners of the company, respectively. The top half lists everything the company owns, and the bottom half lists everything it owes.

One thing you will notice is that the number listed for **total assets** matches the number listed for **total liabilities and shareowners' equity.** *This is always true.* Assets *always* equal liabilities plus equity. Period, end of sentence. That's why it's called a balance sheet. The company will always owe exactly as much as it owns. That means that every increase or decrease in the amount of assets must be matched by an equal change in liabilities and/or equity. It's a law, like the conservation of energy in physics.

Remember that a corporation is a fictional legal entity that is set up by investors for the purpose of conducting business. When the company is first formed, all of the assets are provided by the investors, and the corporation owes the investors for these assets. Later, the company may borrow funds from outside creditors, which also must be accounted for. So, whatever funds are put in or taken out must be reflected somewhere on the balance sheet.

Hold on, you say. What happens when the company earns a profit on the sales of its product? Assets go out, but more comes in than went out. That is true, but keep in mind that the profit belongs to the investors who own the company, so the excess cash generated from the sale is shown as being owed to the shareowners. Therefore, everything pumped into it is owed to someone: either to the investors or to other outside creditors.

Every dollar that comes in or goes out must be accounted for. This is a law of accounting that can never be broken:

$$Assets = Liabilities + Equity$$

The second law to keep in mind when reading the balance sheet is that assets are valued according to what they cost originally (minus accumulated depreciation, which will be explained later), not necessarily what they might be worth at the time you are reading the report.

Assets

We will concentrate on the assets section (more so than liabilities) because that is the arena where improvements to the company's operations will probably show themselves.

The assets section is divided into two principal parts: **current assets** and **property**. (In other balance sheets the latter section may be called **long-term assets** or **fixed assets**). The best way to understand the difference between the two categories is to consider the basic workings of a business. In the discussion to follow we will concentrate on a traditional manufacturing company, rather than a retail or service company.

When the company is first formed, it needs certain things in order to begin its operations. These assets may include manufacturing equipment, land and buildings in which to house the equipment, desks and chairs for administrative workers, computers, vehicles, and the like. They are called fixed assets or long-term assets because they are generally located in one place and are expected to have long, productive lives. You can think of the fixed assets as the infrastructure of the company.

The business will also have a certain amount of **cash** on hand, with which to purchase raw materials, pay staff and line workers, pay rent, and so on. Cash is an **operating asset**—it is used to sustain, and is created by, ongoing operations. Cash shown on the company's balance sheet is not limited to currency on hand, but may include checking accounts, short-term investments, and other financial instruments.

As business operations begin, raw materials are purchased; manufacturing, processing, or assembly procedures are conducted; and finished goods are prepared for sale to customers. These raw materials, work in process, and finished goods together comprise the company's **inventory**. The formal definition of inventory is assets held by the company with the express intention of sale.

As inventory is sold, customers generally are allowed to purchase on credit, paying for the inventory that they receive within about 30 to 60 days. The funds that are owed to the company in consideration for products sold are shown on the company's books as **accounts receivable**.

As you may have guessed, cash, inventory, and accounts receivable are all classified as operating assets because they are created as a result of ongoing business operations. Another name for these operating assets is **current assets**. Formally, any asset that either is cash or is expected to be converted to cash within one year is considered a current asset. Although the company will typically own inventory before it can create accounts receivable, receivables are listed first on the balance sheet because *current assets are listed in order of liquidity, or how readily they can be converted to cash.*

You will often see a final category under current assets. On the sample balance sheet, it is listed as **other current assets**, but you might also see the term **prepaid expenses**. These are payments the company has made for a year's worth of services, such as insurance. As you will see later, most of the performance improvements you will be able to provide your customer through the application of your product will affect the current assets.

In a nutshell, that is an explanation of most of the asset categories shown on the balance sheet. However, you should also be aware that as the company continues operations over a number of years, some other categories will crop up within the long-term assets listing.

Note the term **accumulated depreciation** which is subtracted from total property. You will recall that assets are shown on the books at cost, which is the value that the company paid for them originally. In real life, however, assets typically lose value from the first day they are used, through normal wear and tear, obsolescence, and so on. Every asset has an estimated useful life, and the total cost is divided by the estimated useful life in order to arrive at a figure which is deducted from the value of the assets every year. (Why would a company want to deduct the value of its assets from the books and decrease earnings? Simply put, it's a way to reduce its tax liability even though the money does not actually flow out of the company.) Therefore, **net property** is theoretically the value of the property on today's market. This value is known as the **book value**. In reality the figure is computed from tax tables and may bear little or no relation to the actual **market value**. You will see more on this later.

Another term you must understand is **intangible assets**. As the term implies, these are not hard assets which can be touched or seen, but that does not mean they have any less value. Intangible assets include patents, capitalized research-and-development costs, leasehold rights, and goodwill.

Many of the companies you are working with will have a different look to the balance sheet, depending on the industry. Companies that sell only services, for example, do not show inventory on the books. Retail stores that sell only to consumers do not have accounts receivable. Also, there might be differences in terminology, but you can usually figure out which category the items belong to.

Liabilities and Equity

We will not spend too much time on the bottom, or right side, of the balance sheet because most of the people you will be dealing with in the customer's organization are primarily concerned with the left side, the assets. The asset side of the balance sheet reflects daily operational decisions, while the liabilities side primarily reflects financial decisions. However, it is useful to know the terminology. The funds to purchase or create a company's assets come from two different sources: its creditors and its owners. Funds owed to creditors are called **liabilities**, and funds owed to owners are called **equity**.

Liabilities

Liabilities are listed on the balance sheet in two categories just as assets are: short-term and long-term. Short-term liabilities are those that are payable to creditors within one year, and are usually called **current liabilities**. Figure 4-3, excerpted from the Rockwell International balance sheet, illustrates the various types of liabilities.

Short-Term Debt

Although all current liabilities are short-term debt, the short-term debt category comprises funds owed to banks or other lenders, which are usually for a specified term and are evidenced by a promissory note. Most short-term borrowings are used to supplement short-term cash needs and support buildups of inventory or tide the company over until accounts receivable are collected. This account is frequently listed as **notes payable**.

Accounts Payable—Trade

When the company purchases goods from its suppliers, it does not have to pay immediately. Accounts payable are those funds owed to suppliers of the company for goods or services received that have not yet been paid for.

Accrued Compensation and Benefits

Sometimes the company will receive services before it has paid for them. For example, salaries and commissions will accrue until they are paid at the end of the pay period.

Current liabilities		
Short-term debt	$ **66**	$ 323
Accounts payable—trade	**840**	801
Accrued compensation and benefits	**436**	391
Accrued income taxes	**96**	155
Other current liabilities	**532**	565
Net liabilities of A&D business	**—**	1,309
Total current liabilities	**1,970**	3,544
Long-term debt	**156**	156
Accrued retirement benefits	**795**	764
Other liabilities	**239**	256

Figure 4-3. Types of Liabilities

Accrued Income Taxes

By the time the company has calculated its profits for the year, it typically has some time before income tax payments are due to the government. This represents the accrued amount.

Other Current Liabilities

Other current liabilities may include **current maturities of long-term debt** which is the portion of long-term debt principal payments due within one year.

Long-Term Liabilities

Long-term liabilities are the debts that the company must pay in the future after one year. Examples are mortgages and bonds. If you are really interested in finding out what they consist of, you can refer to the fine print in the notes to financial statements.

Equity

The equity accounts represent the funds invested in the business by its stockholders. The excerpt of the Rockwell equity accounts shown in Figure 4-4 demonstrates the concepts.

To understand the various equity accounts, we must trace the funding of the business from the time of the initial public offering (IPO) of the company's stock. We will concentrate on only three categories: common stock, additional paid-in capital, and retained earnings.

When the company decides to issue shares to the public in order to raise capital, it will select an investment banking firm which will help it structure the stock offering, write a prospectus (business plan) to

Shareowners' equity

Common stock (shares issued: 1997, 216.4 million; 1996, 209.5 million)	**$216**	$210
Class A common stock (shares issued: 1996, 27.9 million)	—	28
Additional paid-in capital	**901**	199
Retained earnings	**4,409**	4,466
Currency translation and pension adjustments	**(103)**	(103)
Common stock in treasury, at cost	**(612)**	(544)
Total shareowners' equity	**4,811**	4,256

Figure 4-4. Equity Accounts

describe the business to potential buyers, and place a projected value on the stock, based on projected earnings and many other factors.

Suppose that the company decides to issue 1 million shares at a **nominal value** (the value shown on the face of the stock) of $10 per share. This price is known as the **par value**. If it sells at that price, it will bring in $10 million to the company (minus the fees charged by the investment bankers). This will show up on the balance sheet as common stock. On the asset side, of course, cash will increase by $10 million to keep things in balance.

If the underwriters did a very good job selling the company's stock, or if the stock market was hot at the time of the IPO, then the company's stock would probably sell for more than the par value. There have been some notable examples of this lately, especially with high-tech stocks such as Netscape and Genentech. The amount brought in excess of the par value is shown on the balance sheet as additional paid-in capital.

Of course, the shareowners will expect that the company's business operations will turn a profit. When the company does earn a profit, it can do two things with it: it can give the profits to the shareowners in the form of dividends, or keep the profits in the company and reinvest them. Most mature companies will do some of each, retaining some earnings and paying some out as dividends. When a company is growing quickly and needs as much capital as possible to sustain growth, or when things are not going well, it will not pay dividends. Profits kept in the business are called **retained earnings**. The retained earnings account will continue to increase while the company is earning profits. When it loses money, the retained earnings account will decrease by that amount.

THE INCOME STATEMENT

We now turn to the most important section in the company's financial statements. Because it measures the performance of the business executives you meet, it's essential that you know it intimately. The income statement is the true scorecard by which managers are measured today. It is where the results of their decisions show up in unforgiving black and white. It is where bonuses are won or lost, and careers are made or broken. It is also the scorecard by which existing or potential shareholders settle on the ultimate measure, the company's stock value.

More to the point, the income statement is a very useful place to look for profit-improvement opportunities. There is a lot of detail between the top line and the bottom line of the income statement, and each line may offer clues for ways to improve the company's business operations.

Because it is so important to the business managers to whom you will be selling, you must know intimately the structure and dynamics of your customers' income statements. It's like using the statistics from the previous season to gauge the various facets of a sports team's performance.

Note: Just because they like to confuse salespeople, various companies will use different names for this section of the financial statements. Other names you will see include:

- (Consolidated) Statement of Operations
- (Consolidated) Statement of Earnings

The Accrual Method of Accounting

As you begin to study your customers' income statements, keep in mind that these tables do not always accurately reflect the true inflows and outflows of cash during the period. Most income statements are presented using the accrual method of accounting. This simply means that revenues and expenses are credited to the period in which the transaction took place, not when the funds actually changed hands. For example, the revenue for a product shipped in December would be credited in that year, even if the customer does not pay until the following year.

Structure of the Income Statement

The balance sheet was described as a snapshot taken at a particular point in time (the end of the fiscal year, in the case of the annual report). The income statement, on the other hand, is more like a movie. It shows the cumulative results of the millions of transactions that took place during the year.

The premise of the company's income statement is straightforward: it shows how much revenue the company brought in, how much it spent, and how much it kept at the end of the year as profit. This gives us the basic income statement equation:

$$\text{Revenues} - \text{Expenses} = \text{Profit}$$

Although this is very simple to understand, accountants make it a little more complicated. They show expenses in specific categories that reflect how the company actually operates. If you can understand these categories, you can understand the dynamics of how the company earns a profit, which can help you find ways to improve its processes.

To become familiar with the various parts of the income statement, let's use the example in Figure 4-5. As you can see, the income statement is very general and high level. It gives you figures from a companywide perspective, so it does not provide much detail about

Consolidated Statement of Earnings
For the years ended October 31

In millions except per share amounts	1997	1996	1995
Net revenue:			
Products	$36,672	$33,114	$27,125
Services	6,223	5,306	4,394
Total net revenue	42,895	38,420	31,519
Costs and expenses:			
Cost of products sold	24,217	22,013	17,069
Cost of services	4,102	3,486	2,945
Research and development	3,078	2,718	2,302
Selling, general, and administrative	7,159	6,477	5,635
Total costs and expenses	38,556	34,694	27,951
Earnings from operations	4,339	3,726	3,568
Interest income and other, net	331	295	270
Interest expense	215	327	206
Earnings before taxes	4,455	3,694	3,632
Provision for taxes	1,336	1,108	1,199
Net earnings	$ 3,119	$ 2,586	$ 2,433
Net earnings per share	2.95	2.46	4.63
Weighted average shares and equivalents outstanding	1,057	1,052	526

The accompanying notes are an integral part of these financial statements

Figure 4-5. Sample Income Statement

specific business segments or product lines. But it can be a useful starting point to help you put your finger on various trends and suggest clues for deeper research.

The income statement shown here indicates the total amount of revenue that flowed into the company during 1997 and the prior two years. It also shows you the bottom-line profit that the company earned for the entire year, as well as relating that figure to the number of shares outstanding.

These are the most important measures for the primary audience of annual reports: potential or actual stockholders. However, all of the categories in between the top and bottom lines are the ones that should be of most interest to you, as the salesperson looking for ways to improve profits for your customer.

Of all the expenses that a company must subtract from revenues, there are three general categories:

- The cost to prepare the product for sale, the **cost of goods sold**
- Expenses associated with running the company, **administrative expenses** (overhead)
- **Financing expenses** the company must pay for the money it uses

To illustrate these categories, let's review the basic business operations that are summarized in income statements. Once again, this discussion assumes a typical manufacturing operation, rather than service or retail.

Net Revenue

The total amount of money paid by customers for goods purchased from the company is shown as net revenue. The reason it does not say *gross* revenue is that typically a company will give back money to customers in the form of discounts, returned goods, and so forth, but these do not normally show up on the income statement.

Cost of Products Sold

In order to have goods available for sale, the company must buy inventory, and then build, shape, assemble, cut, change, or add to it in some way. This requires the use of machines, energy, supplies, movement of goods, and labor to pay the folks who actually do the work. All of the expenses of acquisition plus those directly caused by the manufacturing or assembly operations can be directly tied to the inventory. They are shown on the sample income statement as cost of goods sold, but you may also see "cost of sales."

The difference between the net revenue and the cost of goods sold is the **gross profit**, although most income statements do not explicitly show that figure. More important than the actual gross profit is the **gross profit margin**, which is the percentage of sales represented by gross profit.

Note: whenever you see the term *margin*, always think *percentage*. It is a number arrived at by dividing the number in question (in this case, the gross profit) by the net revenue. For example, if revenue is a dollar, and cost of goods sold is $60, gross profit is $40. The gross margin in this case is 40 percent, which is gross profit divided by net revenue.

Gross profit can be viewed as a good measure of the value the company adds to its customers, because it indicates the amount customers are willing to pay over and above the cost to produce the items.

The cost of goods sold is generally a variable cost, because the amount varies in proportion to the volume of production.

Selling, General, and Administrative Expenses

Another category of expenses comprises the costs associated with running the company on a daily basis, including administrative salaries, sales commissions, advertising, rent, telephone expenses, and all the thousands of other miscellaneous costs that must be paid to keep the company running. Obviously this category encompasses literally hundreds of different categories of expenditures, and the annual report will not give you the detail you might need to determine specific problem areas.

Selling, general, and administrative expenses will sometimes be shown by their abbreviation, SG&A, or more often, as **operating expenses**. They are fixed costs, because regardless of how much is produced by the company (within a certain range, of course), these costs must still be paid.

Subtracting operating expenses from gross profits yields income from operations, or **operating income**. This is a critical number on which to focus, because it is the single best measure of how effectively and efficiently the company runs its business operations. The other expenses that follow after these are due to financing, taxes, and extraordinary events which are typically out of the control of the operating managers to whom you will be selling.

To differentiate operating income from other expenses, they are shown separately. The two principal expenses left to pay are **interest**, which is due on the company's financial obligations, and **extraordinary income or expense**.

Extraordinary, or nonrecurring, income or expense is reserved for charges that do not occur in the ordinary course of business and are not expected to be regular expenses. Examples include disposal of assets, charges associated with changes in accounting standards, and legal settlements.

Net Earnings

One final bite must be taken out of the revenue pie: taxes. Once all expenses are subtracted the company can calculate its tax burden. The final number left is **net earnings**.

The last two lines simply relate net earnings to the number of shares outstanding, so shareholders can compute directly how the company's earnings affect them.

The step diagram in Figure 4-6 summarizes the various levels in the typical income statement.

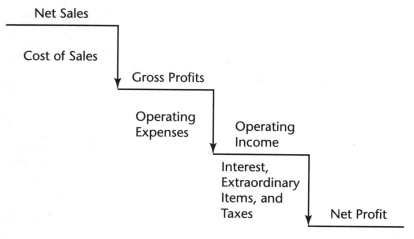

Figure 4-6. Steps in a Typical Income Statement

THE STATEMENT OF CHANGES IN FINANCIAL CONDITION

The final section of the financial statements has the longest name but is of least interest to salespeople. Here is just a short explanation of that form so you will know what it is.

Remember, the balance sheet is a snapshot taken at the end of each year. The income statement is a movie showing what happened during the year. Remember also that the income statement is done on an accrual basis, which means that transactions are reported even if cash does not change hands. Sometimes the reverse is true: cash changes hands but there is no transaction shown on the income statement. Because "cash is king" (we will prove that in Chapter 7), the statement of changes in financial condition keeps track of what happened to all that cash during the year.

WHERE WE GO FROM HERE

In this chapter you have learned the definitions of the various items shown on the financial statements. Having that knowledge should give you the confidence to discuss business issues with your customers' high-level decision makers.

This is really only a start. Unlike accountants, salespeople know that the numbers are not reality. They merely reflect the results of thousands of business operations, many of which we might be able to improve for our customers to make the scorecard look better.

The next chapter shows you how to find meaning behind the numbers in order to uncover profit-improvement opportunities.

ACTION POINTS

After you have looked up a word in the dictionary, the best way to retain it is to use it in a sentence several times. In the same vein, you should get annual reports for your top three customers or prospects and fill in the following table. This will give you practice in locating the information you need and help you learn a little more about your customers.

Customer: _____ _____ _____

Total Assets			
Shareowners' Equity			
Total Liabilities			
Current Assets			
Cash			
Accounts Receivable			
Inventory			
Fixed Assets			
Accounts Payable			
Current Liabilities			
Revenue			
Gross Profits			
SG&A Expenses			
Operating Income			
Net Income			

5

Making Sense of the Numbers

When you take your car to a garage, the mechanic will connect your engine to certain diagnostic tools to spot potential problems instead of immediately proceeding to take it apart. This saves the mechanic a lot of time, and you a lot of money. If you think of your customer's business operations as a vast engine dedicated to producing cash, you can use similar tools to diagnose and tune your customer's *cash flow engine*. This chapter will show you how to use some simple measurements to help you spot opportunities for improvement in your customer's business performance. These measurements will help you zero in on potential problem areas, frame the right questions to ask your buyers, and even suggest possible solutions.

By themselves, the numbers on the financial statements don't mean much; they make sense only in relation to other numbers. For example, suppose you did not know anything about baseball. If you were told that a hitter had a .317 average, you would not have a clue what that meant unless you could compare that statistic with other hitters' batting averages. You would also have to know a little about how the game is played.

To gauge the performance of a business, you will use the same principles that sports fans do. The analysis of company financial statements is as simple as comparing sports statistics or any other types of analysis you do everyday. Financial types call it *ratio analysis*. A ratio is simply one number divided by another, like the number of hits divided by the number of times at bat. The key, of course, is to know which measurements are important and what they tell you about a company's performance.

As you calculate the ratios in this chapter, the numbers you end up with will make sense only when you have something to compare them against. Because there is no absolute standard for any of the measures, they make sense only relative to the firm's performance against its peers and against its historical performance. *Comparative analysis* compares the firm's performance against that of similar firms for a particular time period; *trend analysis* analyzes the firm's performance over time.

Knowing a few simple measurements will help you pick out nuggets of specific meaning from the mass of numbers in the financial statements and enable you to isolate specific areas of performance improvement. This is going to help you in several ways:

- It will improve the quality of the questions you ask your customers about their business, and better questions will give you better answers. Although prospects like to talk about themselves and their business, they expect you to have a basic level of knowledge. Remember when they told you in school that there is no such thing as a stupid question? That's not true in sales. Buyers simply don't have time to spend educating salespeople.
- The improved quality of your questions will signal your business competence and earn you the right to talk to higher-level decision makers. It will boost your credibility by showing that you care enough to do your homework.
- It will save you time. You will have the ability to diagnose potential customer problems faster, helping you target the real problem owners within the client's organization. This is extremely important because of the final point:
- *The buyer does not always know where the true problems are.* Finding clues in customers' financial statements and being able to demonstrate that you have solved similar problems for other customers will help you "create the pain" and "sell them the aspirin."

WHAT YOU NEED TO KNOW

Unlike financial analysts, who must be concerned with the company's balance-sheet structure as well as its operations, as a salesperson you will focus primarily on your customer's income statement and pay just a bit of attention to the assets.

To aid in your search for profit-improvement opportunities, you will use two basic types of measurements:

- Operating ratios
- Activity ratios

Operating Ratios

A company's income statement is the scorecard that sums up all the business activities and indicates success or failure for the year, so it is the first place to look for profit-improvement opportunities. You can learn a lot about how a company has performed if you focus on just a few principal components of its income statement and ask some fundamental questions about each.

Think of a company's income statement as a pipeline like the one depicted in Figure 5-1. The firm takes in revenue at one end, and profit issues from the other end. Usually the profit that comes out is a very small percentage of the total revenue that went in. Obviously most of the revenue leaks out in the form of expenses. There are three major "leaks," or expense categories, that accountants use to make the income statement easier for management and investors (and salespeople) to understand. As you saw in Chapter 4, these major expense categories are cost of goods, oper-

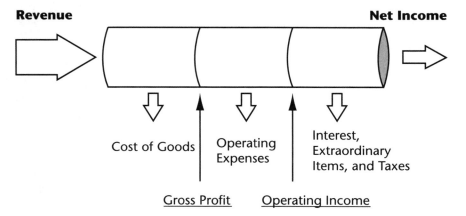

Figure 5-1. The Revenue Pipeline

ating expenses, and a catch-all category comprising interest, extraordinary items, and taxes. The amounts left over at the end of each stage are known as gross profits, operating income, and net income, respectively.

With this visual model in mind, let's take a look at each of the categories of the income statements and ask some fundamental questions about each. For this discussion, we will work with the actual income statement for Sun Microsystems, depicted in Figure 5-2.

You might notice right away that the Sun income statement does not exactly follow the neat pattern depicted in Figure 5-1. Many income statements are expressed slightly differently from the model, but it is easy to make the adjustment. Simply subtract cost of sales from net revenues to calculate gross profits. To make more sense of the income statement, the next thing we will do is convert the numbers to percentages (margins).

Converting Numbers to Percentages: Calculating Margin

Margin is a way of expressing any number on the income statement *as a percentage of total revenues.* This will help you compare the income statement performance of different-size companies.

Consolidated Statements of Income For the years ended June 30 In millions except per share amounts	Sun Microsystems		
	1997	**1996**	**1995**
Net revenues:	**$8,598**	$7,095	$5,902
Cost of sales	**4,320**	3,921	3,336
Research and development	**826**	653	563
Selling, general, and administrative	**2,402**	1,788	1,503
Nonrecurring charges	**23**	58	—
Operating income	**1,027**	675	500
Interest expense	**(7)**	(9)	(18)
Interest income	**40**	43	41
Gain on sale of equity investment	**62**	—	—
Income before income taxes	**1,121**	709	523
Provision for income taxes	**359**	232	167
Net income	**$ 762**	$ 477	$ 356
Earnings per common and equivalent share	**1.96**	1.21	.91
Weighted average common and common equivalent shares	**389**	393	394

Figure 5-2. Sample Income Statement

Using this concept, net revenues are always equal to 100 percent. Gross profit margin is gross profit divided by net revenues; net margin is net income divided by net revenues; and so on. Put another way, margin tells you how many cents out of every dollar of sales are left after each category of expenses is deducted. For example, a gross profit margin of 42 percent means that, after deducting the cost of goods sold, the firm has 42 cents left out of every sales dollar. A 5 percent net margin means that the firm kept five cents out of every sales dollar after paying all expenses.

Margin is a specific financial term. Whenever you hear the word *margin*, think *percent*. In Figure 5-3, the Sun income statement has been redone, adding the relevant percentages. (This is called "common-sizing.")

Notice that calculating the margins helps to clarify the income statement, by making it easy to compare one year with the next. (It also makes it easy to compare Sun's performance with that of other companies.)

Consolidated Statements of Income For the years ended June 30 In millions except per share amounts	1997	%	1996	%	1995	%
Net revenues:	$8,598	100	$7,095	100	$5,902	100
Cost of sales	4,320	50.2	3,921	55.3	3,336	56.5
Research and development	826	9.6	653	9.2	563	9.5
Selling, general, and administrative	2,402	27.9	1,788	25.2	1,503	25.5
Nonrecurring charges	23	.3	58	.8	—	
Operating income	1,027	11.9	675	9.5	500	8.5
Interest expense	(7)	.1	(9)	.1	(18)	.3
Interest income	40	.5	43	.6	41	.7
Gain on sale of equity investment	62	.7	—		—	
Income before income taxes	1,121	13.0	709	10.0	523	8.9
Provision for income taxes	359	4.2	232	3.3	167	2.8
Net income	$762	8.9	$477	6.7	$356	6.0
Earnings per common and equivalent share	1.96		1.21		.91	
Weighted average common and common equivalent shares	389		393		394	

Figure 5-3. Sample Income Statement with Margins Calculated

Analyzing Operating Performance

Next we must decide which numbers are relevant to understanding the customer's business performance. Figure 5-4 returns us to the revenue pipeline, with a recommended order in which to look at your client's income statement. Following these five steps will enable you to see the big picture and gradually focus on specific issues and opportunities for improvement.

The amount of net profit your customer ends up with is the result of literally thousands of business operations and decisions made during the year. The more you know about what affects the amount of revenue received and the "leakage" at each stage, the easier it will be to find ways to help the customer end up the year with more flowing out of the pipeline.

Let's take a look at each of the five steps in more detail. As you read the following pages, you may refer to the common-size Sun income statement in Figure 5-3 or use one of your customers' income statements.

Step 1: Revenue

Let's start first with the top line to see how sales are going. This figure shows the total revenues earned, minus sales returns and discounts from list price. Just as with all the other numbers on the statement, however, there is more to this figure than meets the eye. You need to know the detail and the reasons behind it.

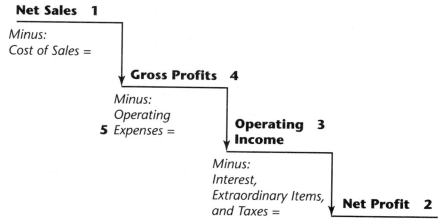

Figure 5-4.   How to Look at the Income Statement

How much did revenues increase or decrease over the previous year?

As you sell to high-level decision makers within companies, you will probably notice a greater concentration on revenue-improvement opportunities than in the past. For the last decade or so, the focus in American business has seemed to be primarily directed at cost cutting, improving efficiency, and reengineering. While this focus has had some success in making companies leaner and more efficient (and caused a lot of pain along the way), companies are beginning to realize that they cannot cut costs forever. Naturally efficiency will always be important, because companies are not about to give up the hard-won gains they have achieved, but the mind share generated by revenue concerns will probably be greater than it has been in the past. Revenue growth is affected by many considerations, including:

- Market acceptance versus competitors
- Innovation
- New markets
- Pricing decisions
- Marketing and sales effectiveness
- Industry trends
- The state of the economy
- Acquisitions or divestitures

As you examine Sun's (or your own customer's) income statement, try to answer the following questions:

1. Was the company's growth faster or slower than that of its competitors?
2. What were the reasons for the company's either outperforming or underperforming its peers?
3. How did sales growth compare with the previous year. Is growth accelerating or declining?
4. What percent of the market does the company control, and how has that changed?
5. Where does that place it within its industry?
6. What are the prevailing industry growth trends?
7. Were changes in revenues caused by more units sold (volume) or higher prices?

8. Were changes in revenues caused by acquiring or divesting operating units, or opening or closing more locations?
9. How do changes in revenues reflect changes in the mix or type of product sold?
10. What new products were introduced, and how did they perform relative to expectations?

Looking at Sun's performance in Figure 5-3, we see that net revenues went up substantially, from $7.1 billion to $8.6 billion. The increase is 21 percent, which is excellent growth, although we could check Sun's competitors to see how much they grew. So far, so good.

Step 2: Net Income (or Net Margin)

Next, skip down to the net income. This is the proverbial bottom line. How much of total revenues did the company manage to keep? While revenue growth is important, it's not how many pennies you begin with that counts, but rather how many are left in the pile after everybody has been paid. Therefore, the net margin figure (net income as a percentage of total revenues) is more useful. Ultimately the price of the company's stock will depend on the company's earnings performance.

Did net margin increase or decrease?

As impressive as Sun's revenue growth was, its net income growth of 60 percent was even better. Its net margin increased from 6.7 percent to 8.9 percent. Based on the evidence so far, Sun seems to have done pretty well in 1997, and no problems are apparent. However, there are literally thousands of expense categories that affect net income, so we need to take the next three steps and see how well this observation holds up.

Step 3: Operating Income (or Operating Margin)

Although net income is closely watched by financial analysts and investors, you should focus more closely on your customer's operating income. It is the single best measure of how well the firm conducted its daily business operations. You can see from Figure 5-3 that Sun's operating income is what is left over from operations *before* subtracting nonoperational expenses. These include interest, taxes, and extraordinary income or expense. While these factors affect the bottom line, they are not usually within the daily control of the operating managers of the business that you will deal with. For example, after the merger mania of the 1980s, many otherwise sound companies with healthy operating income showed minimal earnings or even losses. This is because most of their operating profits went to pay the heavy debt service on the loans that were taken out to buy the company. Although this was not the case with Sun, for many such firms the company's net income would not be a very reliable indicator of the operational health of the company. Unless you are selling financial instruments or loans, the effect of your solutions will show up only in operating earnings.

Here is the operating margin calculation:

$$\text{Operating Margin} = \frac{\text{Operating Income}}{\text{Net Revenues}}$$

Of course, the operating margin by itself does not mean much until you compare it with the margins of other companies and the company's own historical performance. If you spot potential problems, you can then look in the two principal expense categories: cost of goods and administrative expenses.

Note: one of the difficulties with this approach is that the company you are selling to might be involved in several different industries, so it can be tough to get specific numbers for the division you are working with. Sometimes that information is buried in the fine print of the annual report. You may also find the information in analysts' reports, which are explained in the following chapter.

In Sun's case the 1997 operating margin was 11.9 percent, as compared with 9.5 percent the prior year. That represents impressive improvement, especially given the strong growth in revenues. What was the reason for this improvement?

Step 4: Gross Profit (or Gross Profit Margin)

If a company's operating margin indicates performance deficits or improvements (in comparison either with other companies or with its own historical performance), the reason will be found in either its gross profit margin, its operating expenses, or both.

Gross profit is the amount left over after paying for the direct costs to produce the products. These are the earnings a company must use to support its overhead and all administrative functions.

Gross profit and gross profit margin are the best measurements of the amount of value a company adds to its customers. The concept is pretty simple: a firm takes in raw materials, adds value to them, and then lets the market determine how much value was actually added. Higher gross profit margins indicate higher relative value, and lower gross profit margins indicate lower relative value. In the same way, the amount your customers are willing to pay for your product is a function of the amount of value they perceive. In many ways, gross profits are a better measure of growth than revenues. After all, it is a fairly simple matter to increase sales by reducing prices, but that is not a true indication of the company's effectiveness in that market.

The income statement does not always list gross profit directly, but it is easy to calculate. Simply subtract cost of goods sold from revenues. As you can see on the Sun income statement, there is not a separate line item showing gross profits, but all you have to do is subtract cost of sales of $4.32 billion from net revenues of $8.598 billion, for gross profits of $4.278 billion. To arrive at the gross profit *margin,* divide that difference by net revenues:

$$\text{Gross Profit Margin} = \frac{\text{Gross Profit}}{\text{Net Revenues}}$$

Remember, this figure tells you how many cents are left from each dollar of sales after deducting the direct costs to produce the goods. In Sun's case the gross profit margin was 49.8 percent in 1997, which is a big increase from 44.7 percent in 1996. We have found a significant part of our answer right here. Sun demonstrated in 1997 that it could sell much more product at higher profit margins, indicating that it added significant value to its customers. To understand the details, we need to read into its annual report or examine other research that has been done on the company. Although the answers are not immediately obvious, now we can focus our search.

As you regard your customer's gross profit margin, keep in mind the following questions:

1. How did the gross profit margin compare with the prior year?
2. What caused changes in the gross profit margin?

3. How does the company's gross profit margin compare with that of other companies in its industry?
4. Do these differences reflect competitive philosophies or market strategies? (For example, some companies position themselves as low-cost/high-volume producers; at the opposite extreme are the high-value-added premium providers.)
5. How do changes in the gross profit margin reflect changes in the mix of products sold?
6. How did competitive considerations affect the gross profit margin?

Dynamics of the Gross Profit Margin

There are two sides to the gross profit margin coin: what a company is able to charge for its products on the open market, and what it costs to produce goods for sale. While this may seem like an overly subtle distinction, one aspect is a sales and marketing problem, and the other side is a production problem. The true nature of the problem will determine exactly whom you will approach in a prospect's organization, and how you will frame your solution.

Cost of products sold looks at the production aspect of the problem. This is what it costs a company to purchase, process, manufacture, assemble, or otherwise acquire inventory for sale.

For a manufacturing company, it may include the cost of the raw materials purchased, plus any expenses directly related to the production of goods for sale, such as direct labor, energy costs, supplies, and even wear and tear on the machines used. For a retail company, it is the cost of inventory purchased plus freight and any other charges directly related to acquiring and stocking the product.

A service company will not show any cost of products sold, because no inventory is produced.

Factors affecting the cost of goods sold include:

• Changes in raw materials prices
• Efficiencies (or lack of them) in manufacturing

continued

---

continued
- Changing mix of products sold
- New-product introductions
- New markets entered or old markets left
- Quality

Do your contacts in your customer's organization have responsibilities for any of these factors?

The other side of the coin is the *average selling price* of a company's products or services. Entire shelves of books in marketing and economics have been written trying to come to grips with pricing decisions and policy, but here are some of the major issues your customers are struggling with on a daily basis:

- Product mix: from low value added to high value added
- Market positioning and perception
- Relative strength of competitors
- Effectiveness of sales and marketing

The list of factors affecting average selling price is potentially endless. In Chapter 10, "Effectiveness," we look at these factors in much more detail to find as many ways as possible to help our customers increase their gross profit margins.

Step 5: Operating Expenses

Besides the cost of manufacturing or acquiring inventory for sale, the principal costs incurred for keeping an enterprise running and maintaining its infrastructure fall under the heading of operating expenses. Another term for this category is selling, general, and administrative (SG&A) expenses.

The main thing to look out for when comparing operating expenses is how much they grew or shrank in relation to sales. If sales grew 10 percent, but operating expenses grew 12 percent, you would want to know why. In Sun's case sales grew 21 percent during 1997, while operating expenses increased 34 percent.

Here's the calculation (for this example, we ignored R&D and non-recurring charges).

- Operating expenses for 1997 were $2,402
- Operating expenses for 1996 were $1,788
- The difference is $614
- The increase is 614 ÷ 1,788 = 34%

Aha! We have finally detected an issue that is probably of concern to the company's management. While its operating performance looked excellent, a quick analysis discloses that not everything is rosy. The obvious question is Why?, followed quickly by, "What can we do about it?" Our analysis so far does not provide the answer, but it does indicate where to look.

Compare your customer's operating expenses with those of the competition. Are they higher or lower? What are the reasons? A higher expense ratio than the competition is not always bad; it may simply reflect choices made by management. For example, concentrating on service may cause higher administrative costs but allow a company to achieve higher gross profit margins. Make sure you understand the profit structure of the company.

Thousands of expense categories affect operating expenses. The best way to pinpoint specific improvement opportunities is to understand your customers' important business processes. The more you know about how your customers do things, the easier it will be to spot opportunities to help them improve. We look at those processes in detail in Chapter 9, "Efficiency."

Activity Ratios

Imagine two cab drivers: both earn $1,000 per week. With only this information, you would reasonably conclude that they are doing equally well. However, suppose you find out that one drives a new Mercedes and the other drives a 15-year-old Ford Escort. Which of the two is making more productive use of assets?

Your customers are subject to the same question as our two cab drivers. Under today's severe competitive pressures, it is not enough for business managers to improve their performance on the income statement, as measured by operating ratios. These numbers in effect measure the output of the firm, but managers are also being driven to reduce the inputs required to achieve those numbers. The trend is toward "leaner" enterprises with a focus on using as few resources as possible. This movement has given rise to such now-familiar terms as just-in-time inventory, virtual corporations, and outsourcing. The concept is simple: If you can achieve the same level of sales or earnings with half the asset base, you can use the funds that are liberated to make other investments.

For example, transportation companies, such as railroads, long-haul trucking firms, and overnight-delivery companies, have realized that one of the best ways to cut costs and increase revenues is to increase the usage of their vehicles. A truck trailer sitting in a parking lot somewhere is not earning any money, so trucking company managers look for ways to keep them in operation as much of the time as possible. Part of their problem is knowing exactly where the vehicles are at any given moment, and many companies have begun using satellite locators and tracking software to keep track of their trucks. The benefit can be realized in the form of either higher revenues for the assets held, or the ability to sell unneeded assets and use the cash in other productive areas of the business.

Activity ratios are measures of how well your customers use their assets. Typically the ratios they use will relate their most important assets to a relevant measure of output. Therefore you will need to become familiar with the measurements used by the particular type of customer with whom you are dealing. In a labor-intensive industry, asset-efficiency measures will likely be based on numbers of people required to produce a given level of revenue. A heavy industrial business might measure sales or net income relative to total fixed assets.

Here are four of the most common activity ratios:

- Return on assets
- Sales to total assets
- Inventory turnover
- Accounts receivable turnover

Return on assets is a rough measure of how efficiently a firm is using its assets. The equation is:

$$\text{Return on Assets} = \frac{\text{Net Income}}{\text{Total Assets}}$$

Example

Compare the 1997 return on assets for two very similar companies: Ameritech and Bell Atlantic. (Dollar figures in millions.)

	Net Income	Total assets	ROA
Ameritech	$2,296	$25,339	9.1%
Bell Atlantic	$2,455	$53,964	4.6%

Which of the two is more efficient in the use of its assets?

Which do you think would be more likely to be interested in a leasing program? (In certain leases, the assets do not show up on the company's books.) *Bell Atlantic has a lower ROA, so an appropriate lease structure could bring in additional profits without adding to assets on the books.*

Sales to total assets is another measure of how efficiently a company is using the assets it has. The equation is written just as it sounds:

$$\text{Sales to Total Assets} = \frac{\text{Sales}}{\text{Total Assets}}$$

Example

Sales to total assets for three aerospace companies are as follows:

Boeing	1.20
Lockheed-Martin	.99
AlliedSignal	.95

Using the same logic as in the previous example, Lockheed-Martin would have had an additional *$4.9 billion* to play with had it been able to match the asset efficiency of Boeing (all other things being equal).

Inventory turnover measures how much inventory is required to keep operations running smoothly. Every company selling a product requires a certain level of inventory on hand to satisfy customer demand, but it costs money to have goods sitting on the shelves. The more often inventory turns over relative to sales, the more efficient the firm.

$$\text{Inventory Turnover} = \frac{\text{Cost of Goods Sold}}{\text{Average Inventory}}$$

As an example, a company having $1 million in cost of goods sold and inventory of $200,000 would have an inventory turnover of five times.

The higher the turnover, the more efficiently the firm is managing its inventory.

Example

In 1997 Wal-Mart's inventory turned over 5.3 times, versus Kmart's 2.8 times.

If Kmart had been able to achieve the same inventory turns as Wal-Mart, it would have freed up almost *$2.9 billion*, which could have been used to open new stores, advertise more, acquire a competitor, and so forth.

Suppose you were trying to sell a database application to allow Kmart to get a better handle on its inventory: would this nugget of information be helpful? *It would certainly help you catch somebody's attention!*

Another way to look at the efficiency of inventory management is to calculate the **days inventory** on hand. This number calculates how long it would take the company to run out of inventory if it continued to sell at the same pace without replenishment. Simply take the number of days in a year divided by the turnover. So, if inventory turns over five times in one year, there are approximately 72 days of inventory on hand. In this case the lower the number of days, the more efficient the company. That means that the cash that would normally be tied up in inventory can be put to more productive uses. You will learn how to help your customer increase the turnover of its inventory and other assets in Chapter 11, "Speed."

Accounts receivable turnover is calculated the same way, except that the top line is total sales and the bottom line is accounts receivable:

$$\text{Accounts Receivable Turnover} = \frac{\text{Revenues}}{\text{Accounts Receivable}}$$

In the same sense, the days receivable is calculated by dividing 365 by the accounts receivable turnover. The fewer days it takes a company to collect what is owed to it, the faster it can put that money back into circulation to make more money.

OPERATIONAL AND FUNCTIONAL MEASURES

The numbers we have discussed so far in this chapter are financial measures: they are found on all financial statements as required by generally accepted accounting principles (known as GAAP). But many firms have their own measurements that they feel more accurately portray the results of specific business processes and reflect the dynamics of their particular industries.

You might think of these as intermediate measurements: they are the results of the company's business processes that need to be improved in order to achieve the financial targets. For example, a firm might measure ratios such as customer satisfaction, response time, throughput, waste, sales per square foot, returns, or closure rates.

The functional measurements in which you are interested may be used only by the company to which you are selling, or could reflect the results of your application which cut across different companies or even industries. They can be very valuable for a salesperson to know, because while the people you are selling to may have only a remote connection to the overall company bottom line, they definitely have a very direct interest in the activity they control. If you know the individual scorecard by which your prospect is measured, you can more effectively make the case for the value of your solution.

In Chapter 14, "Talking to the Right People," you will see how the position of the person to whom you are talking in the company will dictate which measurements you use to sell your solution.

The value of these functional measurements is that they can actually be predictive rather than historical. Financial measurements reflect only results of past performance. Functional measurements also reflect past performance, but it may be performance that has not yet made its impact felt on the financial statements. They are also valuable to you because as a salesperson, you will often find it easier to measure the impact of your solution at this level. For example, you might show how your product can improve response time to customer complaints through a live demonstration, but the results of such performance improvement are much more difficult to predict.

The emphasis on intermediate measurements is best expressed in a management emphasis that is gaining increasing favor: the balanced scorecard concept, or BSC. The BSC states that managers should keep their eyes fixed on a variety of measurements to ensure the long-term health and growth of their business and prevent an unhealthy stress on a few measurements which could cause distortions in other areas of the business. For example, emphasizing short-term profits could lead managers to neglect expenditures on training their workers to be more competitive in the future. The balanced scorecard is likened to an airplane instrument panel to help business managers stay on course. As outlined by Robert S. Kaplan and David P. Norton in their book *The Balanced Scorecard* (Harvard Business School Press, 1996), BSC measures comprise four areas:

- Financial
- Customer
- Internal
- Learning and growth

It can also be very useful to have a good grasp of the drivers of profitability or the principal concerns of your customer's industry. These can help you home in on the "hot buttons" of the person you are talking to, or at the very least demonstrate knowledge which adds to your personal credibility. Many companies will "benchmark" their performance in specific areas, not only against other companies in their industry but also against the "best in class" for those specific metrics. Specific industry measures include:

- Retail stores: sales or gross profit margin per square foot
- Telephone companies: lines per employee
- Banks: deposits per employee, net interest margin
- Airlines: revenue and cost per seat mile
- Hospitals: cost per bed
- Steel mills: cost per ton produced

The possible measurements are endless. Just make sure that you find out which measurements are important to the decision makers within your customer's or prospect's company.

ACTION POINTS

Although you probably do not have time to conduct an in-depth analysis of each of your customers as explained in this chapter, you should definitely do it for your top three or four customers. The exact number is up to you. (If you have a computer, you can create a spreadsheet to calculate these ratios automatically, using the foregoing formulas.) This will help you tremendously with those customers, but it will also yield a side benefit: you will be much more conscious of the key factors affecting the profitability of each of your customers and prospects. In Chapter 7, you will look into the workings of your clients' cash flow engines and will learn how to help your clients tune those engines for the highest possible profit and cash flow.

As you become more familiar with the techniques and principles discussed in this book, you will be able to plan ahead for using your customers' ratios as a selling tool. You will think of your solutions in terms of the specific company measurements they can affect and then begin to look for those measurements in your customers' and prospects' financial information and in your sales call questions.

Fortunately the knowledge is cumulative. As you become familiar with a specific customer in a particular industry, it becomes much easier to understand other companies in the same industry. Your reputation as an expert in that industry will continue to grow, especially as contacts within companies intermix within the industry.

6

Business Intelligence—Beyond the Numbers

In selling, knowledge is value. At certain levels, your customers are almost inundated with information, including product literature, numerous sales calls, trade publications, and in-house expertise. They probably know a lot already about your product, so if you bring only product knowledge to the table, you are not adding any value, and if you are not adding value, you are not helping your customer. That reduces you and your product to commodity status, with price as your only competitive weapon.

At top-tier levels, your customers know nothing about your product, but they also do not care. They have much larger concerns, and besides, they've hired people to know those things. They know a lot about their own businesses, but they also realize that they must continually find ways to improve in order to survive and grow. The knowledge they are looking for is information about how they can get better, and they will instantly recognize the value of that type of information. If you combine your product expertise with your knowledge of the customer's business operations, you can be in a unique position to deliver that kind of value. This combination actually creates new knowledge, and that knowledge is value.

It's clear you have become valuable to your customers when they call you for advice—not simply about products, but about their plans. The more you know, the sooner you are brought into the planning and decision-making loop, the closer you are to the true decision makers, and the more influence and credibility you will have.

Your knowledge brings real benefit to your clients. The benefit it brings to you is shorter sales cycles, higher margins, and more sales. Knowledge also helps you to be proactive, to suggest courses of action or alternatives that are not readily apparent either to the client or to the competition.

Of course, with all these benefits, there has to be a catch. The catch is that it takes time to acquire the range of knowledge and the level of expertise you need to become a value-added sales professional, time that at first glance might seem better spent in front of customers. It can be extremely difficult under the pressure of short-term quotas to find the time to study and to learn. There is obviously a delicate balance between selling-time and learning-time. On the other hand, the difficulty of acquiring it is what makes it so valuable to you as a sales professional. As they say, if it were easy, anybody could do it. Those who take the time and pay their dues will stand out.

THE ANNUAL REPORT IS NOT ENOUGH

The annual report will give you a wealth of information that you can use to your advantage when dealing with your prospects and customers. However, by only reading your customers' annual reports, you may be selling yourself short, for various reasons:

- It is the most obvious place to look. Your competitor is very likely to also have a copy and has access to the same information. Although chances are that your competitor has not read the material with the same focus and knowledge that you have, you can go several steps further by taking advantage of other sources.
- Annual reports are generally not available for privately held companies. Because these businesses are not required to report to shareholders, they usually do not violate their own privacy or go to the expense of producing one.
- To be truly effective, you may need a broader base of knowledge than is available in the annual report, including industrywide expertise and general business trends and practices. In fact, your knowledge of the industry might help you read the annual report more intelligently.

- Annual reports vary in the level of detail and comprehensiveness. Although there are rules governing what must be included, they leave wide latitude for individual company choice. As you may have noticed when you attempted to answer the 10 questions posed in Chapter 3, not all the answers are in the annual.
- You will also need more narrowly focused information at a level of detail that is simply not available in the annual report.
- A tremendous amount of data, information, and expertise is readily available, especially through Internet sources, to those who know where to look, and it would be silly not to take advantage of it.
- When you read your customer's annual report, you know only as much (if that) as the company does about its problems. Broadening your reach can give you access to information that the customer may not have and so make you a valuable resource.

In short, think of the annual report as the admission price to bottom-line selling. It merely gets you in to play the game at the high levels, but it does not ensure success by itself.

THE KNOWLEDGE PYRAMID

Before we dig into the various sources of company information, let's take a look at the different facets of knowledge that, taken together, will make you a true expert and a valuable resource to your customer. Think of the investment opportunity you are offering your customer as the tip of a knowledge pyramid, as shown in Figure 6-1.

The pyramid can be used as a guide for a new salesperson starting out in the profession, or a template for a more experienced professional to fill in gaps or to gain new knowledge. With the pace of change in technology, business, and the world in general, nobody will remain an expert for long without constantly staying on top of the flood of new information available every day.

Generally, the higher you go in the customer organization, and the more expensive your solution, the more your knowledge of the pyramid's lower levels will be tested. At lower levels in the organizational chart, the view is more restricted to product and application questions.

Let's review the building blocks of the knowledge pyramid that support your offer, starting from the bottom and going up.

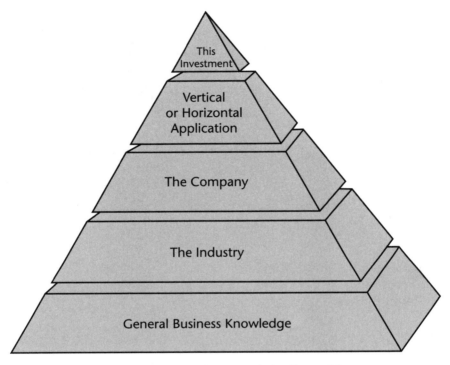

Figure 6-1.   The Knowledge Pyramid

General Business Knowledge

A strong base of general business knowledge can help you in several ways:

- It will give you confidence in your dealings with higher-level business executives.
- It will give you credibility in talking with higher-level business executives.
- A strong grounding in the basics of how businesses function can provide the context for understanding customer problems.
- A knowledge of the latest trends and developments can help you anticipate customer needs.
- It can raise your level of comfort in dealing with a wide range of positions and functions within the customer organization.

General business knowledge is not a static mass of information that you acquire and then have forever. Things are changing so fast that the most important thing is to acquire the habit of being interested in and staying on top of business developments. Here are some suggestions for the sources of this information:

- The *Wall Street Journal*—Reading the *Journal* is probably the best way to stay on top of the latest business news, industry and economic trends, and in-depth company information.
- Recent business books—It's tough to figure out which to read because there are so many of them, ranging from excellent to poor. Generally, if a book makes the bestseller list, you should read it—not because it's necessarily good, but because many of the people with whom you are dealing are likely reading it too. When you start hearing the latest buzzword over and over, there is usually one book that is seen as the "must-read" for that subject. An example is *Reengineering the Corporation,* which introduced the concept of reengineering to the mass business market.[1]
- Business magazines (*Fortune, Forbes, Business Week,* etc.)—These fall between the *Wall Street Journal* and business books in their depth and still give you wide exposure to business trends and company news.
- *Harvard Business Review*—Definitely not for everyone. However, because it generally has cutting-edge articles, on many occasions I have sent copies of articles to clients to alert them to useful information.
- Trade journals—Your customers expect you to be a source of information about your own industry, so keep up with your own trade journals.

The Industry

To understand the issues that confront and perplex the executives with whom you are dealing, it helps to have in-depth knowledge of the customer's industry. How intimately you learn the industry, of course, depends on the range of clients you deal with.

1. Michael Hammer and James Champy, *Reengineering the Corporation—A Manifesto for Business Revolution*, Harper Business, 1993.

If you sell vertical applications and all your clients are in a particular industry, you will want to continuously soak yourself in as much information as possible. In addition to such basics as sources of competitive advantage within the industry and company rankings, you will want to recognize the names of many individuals, industry-specific jargon, latest industry trends, and the like. If your principal focus is horizontal applications that can be used in a wide range of industries, you need the ability to quickly become familiar with the dynamics of a particular industry, the major issues, technological trends, sources of competitive advantage, and principal players.

Every industry has a few basic internal measurements it uses to take the pulse of its business. Make sure you learn the rough rules of thumb that govern the effectiveness of any company in the industry. For example, in the airline industry, it's revenue per available seat mile, and cost per available seat mile. In the cellular telephone industry, executives are intimately concerned with measurements such as churn rate, cost per activation, and average revenue per line. Retailers pay close attention to sales and gross profits per square foot. Knowing these rules of thumb can give you instant credibility. It also becomes helpful to express the benefits of your solution in those terms.

These rules of thumb can often be found in the annual reports, as management discusses its efforts in reaching certain targets. For example, in the 1995 annual report for Federal Express Corporation, management reports its efforts to increase its revenue per package in the face of industry declines in this measure, while pursuing various strategies to drive down its cost per package. However, because these key indicators are internal measurements, they are not always available through the annual reports, and you will have to look elsewhere. Once again, the level of effort you put into this should be proportional to your concentration in a particular industry. Following are other sources of industry-specific data.

Analysts' Reports

Wall Street firms devote a lot of resources to understanding particular industries in an effort to identify winners and losers. Analysts churn out a constant stream of reports about the industries they follow, and these are the most comprehensive sources of information anywhere. A typical industry report prepared by an analyst might run 60 to 70 pages and include industry trends, the critical success factors, competitive analyses and rankings of the key players, and forecasts about future developments.

You may be able to obtain copies from a stockbroker, but the easiest way is to access them through a commercial service. A popular service is InfoTrac, which is available through many local libraries. You can print or download any of the information, and it is usually current to within one or two months. In my experience, there is no other source that contains as much valuable information about a specific industry. *petroleum - Soft Drinks (Coke)*

Industry Sources

Publications

Here are some of the more common publications dedicated to providing industry information, listed in order of comprehensiveness:

- Sources for general business ratios include *RMA Statement Studies*, compiled yearly by Robert Morris Associates from financial reports submitted to banks; *Industry Norms and Key Business Ratios* from Dun & Bradstreet; and *Almanac of Business and Industrial Financial Ratios*, with information compiled from several million federal tax returns.
- *Hoover's Industry Profiles* are available on-line and in printed form.
- Standard & Poor's Industry Surveys are an excellent source if you want in-depth information on a specific industry, with reports ranging up to 50 pages. For example, the most recent survey on the telecommunications industry had eight sections, including basic outlook for the industry, descriptions of conditions in various industry sectors, industry data, and comparative company analyses. The last page had information about relevant trade associations.
- Most industries have their own associations to advance their interests, and they will provide prepared information or answers to specific questions. To obtain a listing of these, consult your local library or the *Encyclopedia of Associations,* or simply ask your customer. Trade associations usually have their own publications,

which can help you immerse yourself in the issues and the jargon of the industry and stay abreast of the latest developments.

All of the publications just listed were available from the medium-size public library in my area. Your company may hold some of the more useful ones in its corporate library.

Partners in the Selling Process (and Other Suppliers)

Many solutions sold today are components in a system of products, which depend on other business partners to make them work. Many of these partners can be helpful sources of information about the specific industries they serve. Use them as a resource, and learn from them. Of course, you may need to exchange information in order to get them to open up. In addition, you might be able to share information with other, noncompetitive, suppliers to that industry or customer.

The Company

Many other sources of information about companies are available besides the annual report. Some have the advantage of being prepared by outsiders, who can be more objective and open about issues the company might rather not discuss. There are also many other documents the company prepares for public consumption that might occasionally be useful:

- Quarterly reports, due 45 days after the end of the quarter, can be very useful as a source of timely information to spot developing trends early. Remember that sometimes the annual report can contain information that is more than a year out of date. In today's highly volatile competitive environment, that can result in very misleading information. When you read the quarterly report, be sure to keep in mind any seasonal variations in sales, in order to make meaningful comparisons. For example, the holiday season causes many companies' fourth-quarter statements to look dramatically different from the first quarter.

- The *Form 10K* is another version of the company's annual report which is filed with the Securities and Exchange Commission. Because the format and content are more restricted, the 10K can usually give you more objective information and a lot less fluff. Sometimes you can also obtain information such as the biographies and compensation plans of top company executives.
- The *Form 10Q* is the quarterly version of the 10K.
- Company publications and newsletters can be very useful to help you spot management changes, upcoming projects and initiatives, business strategies, product announcements, company values, messages from top management, and so on. Often you can pick these up in the lobby or get them from your contacts at the company, or you can even get on the mailing list.
- Press releases can be obtained easily through on-line sources.
- Speeches and statements by company management are generally readily available through your library. *Wall Street Transcripts* regularly publishes the speeches of corporate presidents.
- Most companies now have a home page on the World Wide Web. Sometimes you can find interesting tidbits on them that may not be available elsewhere. Some companies even post notices to prospective vendors explaining how they can do business with the company.

The sales call is also a source—in the end, the best source of relevant information about the company and the needs relevant to your sales opportunity is your contacts within the company. Of course, the quality of the information you receive will be directly proportional to the quality of the questions you ask. Don't rely on this means alone, however. Sometimes you have to earn the right to ask questions, and this requires doing the research beforehand.

Outside Sources

- Analysts' reports—As mentioned previously, the people who know a company best (other than its top managers, although sometimes they can be guilty of seeing what they want to see) are the analysts who devote entire careers to following one company. Their reports are thorough, detailed, and objective. Using a computer database such as InfoTrac, it is common to find up to a dozen reports on a company, ranging from 2 pages to 60. The longer reports probably contain a lot of information that you don't need, but you quickly learn how to scan them for what's relevant to you and discard the rest.

- Media sources—All of the major business magazines have indexes of stories that they have written about companies. You can access these for free through a library, which requires some legwork on your part, or you can order the information from the magazine for a fee.

  You can also call the main newspaper in the city where the company is headquartered and obtain copies of recent articles.

- Your own company files—Sometimes the best information about a company is sitting right in your own company's files. Perhaps another sales rep has dealt with the company in the past and kept reasonable records (don't laugh; it's been known to happen). More likely, someone from a different division within your company has a current or previous relationship with the customer or prospect.

The Corporate Database

The accumulation of customer and industry information does not have to be an individual responsibility, nor should the information and learning accumulated remain at the personal level. In fact, it is extremely important to your whole company that the learning that takes place by individual salespeople in specific accounts be put to good use by the entire organization. When information stays at the personal level, only one person can use and profit from it, and the burdens of collecting the information, developing expertise, and remaining current can be very heavy.

A central repository of customer and industry expertise, which includes account histories, problems faced by customers, records of how your company has solved those problems, and key industry or process measurements that you can impact, can add tremendous value to your sales organization. At the individual level, it helps you to slash the time necessary to become conversant with new opportunities, get up to speed on the constraints and challenges of particular types of problems faced by your customers, find examples of previous successes that can open doors for you at new opportunities, or find the individuals in the organization with specific expertise or insight that may help you with your current prospect.

Sales managers can benefit, principally by resting secure in the knowledge that a valuable corporate asset—intellectual capital—is being preserved and constantly growing in value. Without its being preserved, it is impossible to think of the knowledge as a valuable corporate asset, because it is the type of asset that can be lost forever or even used against the company if the sole owner of the information decides to seek greener pastures. They also know that the learning curve for new sales reps can be significantly shortened, allowing them to begin making contributions to profits much sooner.

Other areas of the corporation can also benefit from the customer knowledge base. Marketing can use the information to structure its approach to the market or for product literature, or to suggest new products. Early information about the problems perplexing customers can help R&D and engineering. Top management may use the information to plan its business strategies and future resource allocations.

Sources for Private Companies

Many of the sources listed are effective only for public companies because outside organizations have a vested interest in publishing information about them. Information about private companies is more limited, but it is still available if you know where to look. Some of the bigger firms may be covered in sources such as *Hoover's Industry Profiles*. For those that are not covered, your best bet is to get as much industry information as possible, because the issues that affect their competitors, as well as their ratios, are probably very close to their own.

The Vertical or Horizontal Application

Vertical applications refer to solutions that apply to a particular industry. For example, you might have an application that works well for the trucking industry. Horizontal applications refer to solutions targeting a specific function that applies to many industries, such as payroll processing, or document management.

Regardless of the appeal of the application, if it has been applied in the past more than once, there is probably something written about it in a trade journal or in your own company literature. *Computerworld*, for example, has regular features on the application of information technology to solve a wide range of problems.

Your own company files and literature, or your colleagues, can be especially useful in describing ways in which to package your product as a solution to specific problems. It does not require too great an imaginative leap to present yourself or your company as a specialist in solving these types of problems. Look for case studies indicating how companies used your product or a similar product, especially focusing on results achieved and benefits realized.

This Investment

The information you need regarding this investment—and where to get it—is the subject of the rest of the book.

USING THE INTERNET

The Internet is no longer a new phenomenon, where you will still be in a privileged minority if you are using it as a tool to boost your selling efforts. By now, you really do not have a choice if you want to be at least as well informed as your competitor. Never in history has so much information been available to those who would take a little time and effort. In fact, there is so much information available that the real trick is to be able to get what you need with minimum effort, and know what it all means. Many of the sources mentioned in this chapter are now accessible almost free and virtually instantly. The best news for busy salespeople is that it does not take long to obtain huge amounts of information, so you don't have to detract from valuable selling time.

As long as you can access the World Wide Web, you can use a search engine to help you find what you are looking for. Some common engines are: Yahoo!, Lycos, AltaVista, and WebCrawler. Any one of these contains a word search function. Just type in the company name, and see what listings are returned. You can then simply double-click on the item you want, and the system will hot-link you directly to the site. That site may also have links to other sources of information, or you can go back to the main browser home page to connect to the next listing.

Many of the leading business publications and newspapers are now on-line and offer a search function to find articles about companies or other business subjects in current and past issues. Using one of the browsers just listed, you can find: *Inc.* magazine, *Fortune, Business Week, Forbes, Investor's Business Daily*, and many others. These are just the free ones. You can also access the *Wall Street Journal* for a fee. Many industry-specific publications and trade magazines are also available.

Other free sites on the Web include:

- Securities and Exchange Commission(www.sec.gov)—This is a must-visit site for electronic copies of required corporate filings, including 10K and 10Q forms. Electronic filing had been voluntary but became mandated by the SEC beginning in January 1998.
- The Motley Fool (www.motleyfool.com)—This is a site designed for investors, but who has a greater interest in having complete information on a company than people investing their own funds? Besides being entertaining in its own right, it provides a search function for companies and industries.

Depending on your budget and depth of interest, many fee-based services on the Internet to which you can subscribe can also be very helpful. What follows is not an endorsement of the specific services, because I have not had the time or inclination to make a detailed study of all the choices. I have found two that work well for me, but the growth of the Web probably means that there are many others.

- Hoover's (www.hoovers.com)—Offers detailed company histories and reports which include markets served, recent financial performance, competitors, and so on. Some limited information is available free of charge, but detailed reports are available only to paid subscribers. This is a useful resource for getting superficially acquainted with a company early in the sales cycle, before you have decided to invest any more time in researching it.

- Market Guide (www.marketguide.com)—A good source for more detailed information about companies. If you are looking for financial ratios to compare your customer or prospect with its peers, this resource will give you up to 50 ratios.

If you want to stay in tune with some of the latest happenings in particular industries or companies, you can also download one of the "push technology" applications such as PointCast. These applications will search out the latest press reports under the subjects you specify and update the information to your computer on a schedule you select. A friend of mine first found out that his boss's boss had been fired when he read it on his computer screen from PointCast!

KEEPING CURRENT

Information has a shelf life, just like fresh milk. You must constantly refresh your knowledge, keeping track of changes in your and your customers' industries, technological trends, major personnel changes, competitive initiatives, new challenges, and opportunities. At least quarterly, you should either request from the company or download from the Internet the company's latest financial results. Many companies will put you on a regular mailing list for their financial information, as well as press releases or announcements. If you specialize in a particular industry, you or your company should own a subscription to the major trade magazines. Depending on budget and time availability, it could also be useful to attend the principal trade shows for your industry and/or your customers' industries, which will not only help you keep up-to-date but help you maintain and widen your network as well.

EXTENDING YOUR KNOWLEDGE

Much of the expertise you pick up will be on an ad hoc basis, adding to your store of knowledge with every sales opportunity you get involved in or hear about from your peers. As long as you face new challenges and opportunities along with your customers, you are bound to keep learning. However, you can take control of your own learning process and proactively increase your own ability to win new business by being selective in your learning and selling opportunities.

First, you must have the mind-set that every sales opportunity, even if not successful, is a chance to add to your knowledge base to make you more effective in the future. If you are successful with one sale to one customer, you will then be in a position to learn more about that customer, which will position you to preserve that relationship and win more business from that account. Next, you may be able to learn more about the particular industry and develop a vertical industry expertise, leveraging off one company to win sales at other similar companies. Or, you can develop your horizontal expertise: using the information gained from successful solutions, you may be able to find more business at other companies, in other industries, that use similar business processes.

The nice part about this whole process is that it continues to become easier, as your success helps your reputation as an expert to spread, which brings you more business and helps you to learn even more. In effect, your customers will be paying you to learn how to make more money for them—and for you.

ACTION POINTS

It is not the point of this chapter that you should turn into a professional researcher. Your primary job is, and always will be, to be in front of customers making sales. You do not have the time to become a "research nerd," knowing everything there is to know about your customers but missing quota every year. There already exist people like that. They're called financial analysts.

Let the analysts do all the work, and you can reap the benefit. Know how to take advantage of the efforts of professional researchers and company analysts and glean from them the nuggets of information that will help you spot sales opportunities, points of entry to a prospect, and ideas to solve customer problems. If you piggyback off their efforts, the expertise you gain will be way out of proportion to the effort put in. A wide range of sources is easily accessible, informative, and free. The trick is to know what to look for and where.

What has been described in this chapter is an ideal. It is highly unlikely that your competitor has achieved this level. But why take chances? I would recommend beginning the process with perhaps your top three customers or prospects and then going on from there as necessary.

Another way to reduce some of the load is to move gradually in your collection of individual company information. Use your judgment, balancing the potential return against the amount of time and effort required. You may order an annual report and a company profile from the Internet, for example, at the beginning stage of your sales effort and then dig further as the opportunity takes shape.

Part 3

Fixing

7

The Cash Flow Engine

Up to this point, we have looked at the results of business activities as they show up on our customers' annual reports and other financial results. It's time to dig deeper: to understand the business processes themselves in order to find ways to improve them. Always keep in mind that the numbers themselves are not reality; they are merely reflections of the customer's business activities and processes. Analogous to a doctor learning how to diagnose the health of a patient, so far we have been studying anatomy. We now turn our attention to physiology—how the parts work together. In this chapter we will look at two models that will help you understand how your customers generate the results that show up in their annual reports: the cash flow engine and the value chain.

THE CASH FLOW ENGINE

A simple yet powerful method for understanding your customer's business is to see it as a vast engine for generating cash. Cash is the central ingredient of any business operation. It is the enabler and the ultimate objective of all the components of the business cycle. Every business both uses and generates cash. It courses through the corporate veins, making all operations possible. (Remember that our definition of cash is broader than mere currency; it includes balances in bank accounts and short-term investments.) In order to understand how the business functions, you must be able to trace the cash flows through the business.

Management pundits (who make their living by complicating simple things) might disagree, but investors know the truth: when you boil down the concept of the business to its bare essentials, its principal mission in life is to *generate cash* for its owners. Investors invest cash in the expectation that it will generate more cash. Only through generating cash will the company be able to dole out dividends to investors, pay salaries, or grow the business. In effect, the entire infrastructure of the business, the legions of employees, the business processes, and all that the enterprise comprises is a vast cash-generating engine:

- The engine is fueled by cash.
- The workings of the engine are lubricated by cash.
- The purpose of the engine is to generate cash.

The key, therefore, to improving the business is to understand how the engine operates, and what it needs to run as effectively and efficiently as possible.

Think of yourself as a cash flow mechanic for a temperamental race car. As you know, auto mechanics get paid for more than the parts they put into the vehicle. They also earn a premium for knowing which parts need repair or replacement, and the good ones do exactly what needs to be done and no more. Race car mechanics take it a step further: besides keeping the engine running, they must constantly search for ways to squeeze better performance out of it in order to gain a competitive advantage.

When you don't know anything about engines, the mass of wires and metal under the hood can seem incredibly mysterious. But when you become familiar with the basic operating principles, it makes sense and quickly becomes very simple and familiar. It's the same way with the workings of a business. As you will see shortly, the core components of the engine are easy to understand, and there are just a few basic routes to performance improvement.

Your job is not to solve all the problems of the business. If you could do that, you would be running it instead of selling to it. Your job is to understand the basic workings of the engine and then apply your imagination and expertise in your particular field to make it better.

Parts of the Engine

The best way to understand the workings of the engine is to build one from the ground up. Ours exists only on paper, but it contains all the parts that a real cash flow engine has.

First, imagine that you have formed a company to sell widgets. Your idea for a new and improved widget, dressed up in a dazzling business plan, has won favor on Wall Street, and they have given you a lot of cash to build widgets—not because they like widgets, but because they like cash. They want you to use that cash to generate even more cash for them. Being an astute investor, you put this cash into a bucket, much like the one in Figure 7-1. It's a perfectly fine bucket, and it contains more cash than you ever dreamed existed in the whole world.

Infrastructure and Cash

There's one problem, though. The bucket has a leak in it. Attached to this bucket and sucking out the cash like a vacuum cleaner is a part of the engine called infrastructure.

In our definition, infrastructure comprises assets such as factories, office buildings, warehouses, equipment, furniture, and supplies. It

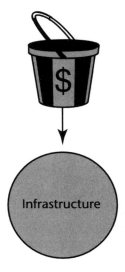

Figure 7-1. Cash Drain from Infrastructure

also includes administrative staff, which in this case means any employee not directly involved in the production or manufacture of widgets. Finally, it includes the financial "infrastructure," the ongoing financial obligations that must be repaid to investors and lenders.

Infrastructure is absolutely essential (yes, even those large staffs) to the running of a business, but it does cost money. Even before the first widget is sold, the infrastructure is using cash. As the operator of the engine, your job is to get some cash flowing back into the bucket to replenish the drain. You have to use some of the cash you have to produce a product for sale, but you cannot use it all; you need to leave some cash in the bucket to run things.

Inventory

In order to refill the bucket, you will produce inventory for sale to the market. Of course, before you can sell inventory, you must first acquire it or make it. This is not a trivial process. If you are going to make a product, you may spend years in dreaming up new products and designing something that will sell in the market. Even after it is designed, prototypes must be built and tested, and factories must be set up to manufacture them. After you reach that point, you must manufacture it:

- Raw materials must be ordered, received, unpacked, inspected, sorted, and delivered to their proper stations or machines.
- The raw materials must have value added to them: this requires sorting, grading for quality, cutting, shaping, bending, painting, sanding, drilling, assembly, and movement from station to station within the factory.
- Finished goods must be inspected, packed, sorted, and prepared for delivery, or stored somewhere until they are sold.

Naturally this is not always a smooth, sequential process. Most of the time, the raw materials and inventory are sitting in piles waiting for value to be added to them. Each of these procedures uses cash and time. While they are taking place, the clock is ticking and cash is draining away. Another problem is that the business is never able to perfectly coordinate its supply and demand, so each "pile" (raw materials, work in process, and finished goods) requires a margin of

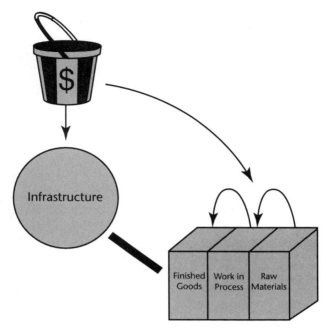

Figure 7-2.   Converting Cash to Inventory

safety. This also uses cash, as shown in Figure 7-2. Every dollar that remains in one of these piles is one that is not being cycled through to generate more cash.

Sales

Next, the inventory must be sold. Unless it is a busy retail operation, this also takes time. As you well know, complex systems sales (such as these widgets—they're digitized and integrated widgets; the marketing department calls them digital widget system solutions) can have a frustratingly long sales cycle:

- Marketing needs to get its message out.
- Salespeople have to prospect and develop relationships.
- Prospects take their time evaluating options.
- Solutions need to be configured.
- Proposals must be prepared.

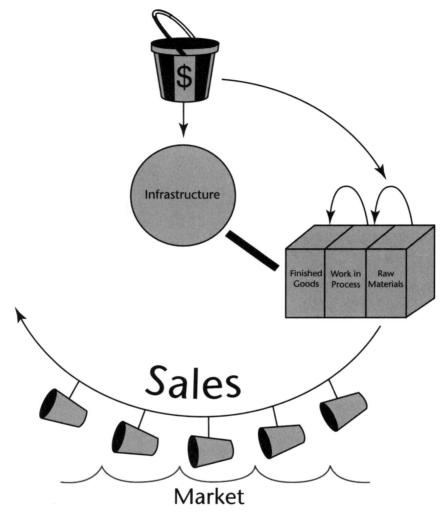

Figure 7-3. Marketing, Selling, and Delivering the Inventory

- Orders must be processed.
- Goods have to be shipped and installed.

Every one of these operations takes time and money (Figure 7-3). And that's just for the *successful* sales efforts. Of course, the payoff is the additional cash that flows back into the company. The more you can charge for your widgets in excess of what they cost to produce, the faster you will refill your cash bucket. The added percentage is called the *gross margin*.

Accounts Receivable

As Figure 7-4 shows, once the goods are delivered, the company must still wait for customers to pay. Until then all they have to show

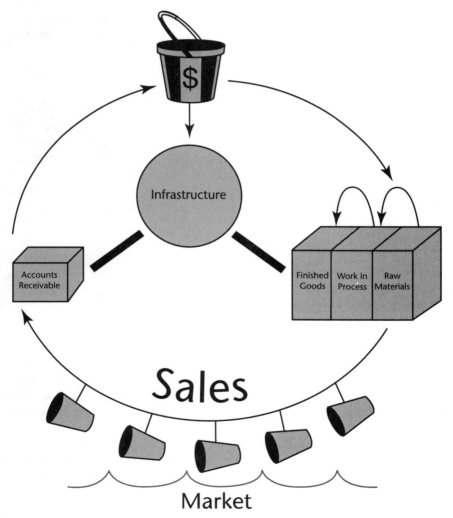

Figure 7-4. Collecting the Money Owed

for their efforts is *accounts receivable*. The company would of course prefer that all its customers pay cash, but they must do what their competitors are doing. In most industries, customers are given *terms*, which means they have a reasonable grace period before they have to pay. Usually the grace period is 30 days, but the terms are sometimes honored more in the breach than in the observance.

Sometimes the company has to make collection efforts and even on occasion write off some bad receivables. Even when payments come in on time, there is usually a delay during which the company processes the payments, deposits the checks, and receives credit for the deposit at the bank.

Profits

At last, the cash begins to flow back into the bucket. Even though you had to leave a lot along the way, in the form of inventory reserves and unpaid receivables, the cash flow engine is beginning to do its job. (See Figure 7-5.) Cash flows back into the bucket and can then be reinvested into the cycle to generate yet more cash.

The accounting difference between what your product cost and what you sold it for is your profit. There are typically three things you can do with your profits:

- Pay dividends to the shareholders.
- Put the profits back into the cycle to generate more cash.
- Put the profits into infrastructure additions or improvements to generate more cash.

Different Engine Types

The model engine built in this chapter depicts the traditional manufacturing company. Your customer might be different. Although the principles remain the same, not all cash flow engines have the same parts.

A service company will have all the parts except inventory.

A retailer has a lot of finished goods inventory, but no raw materials or work in process. It will probably have minimal or no receivables (except credit-card receivables).

An airline has a huge infrastructure, no inventory, and low receivables. The varieties are endless, but the principles remain the same for each.

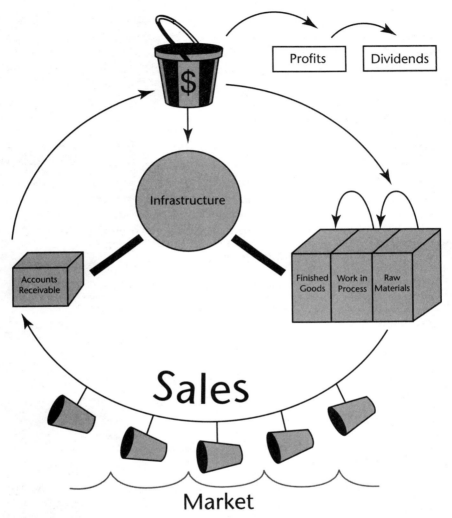

Figure 7-5.   Completing the Cycle: Distributing or Reinvesting Profits

Tuning the Engine

As the engine begins running smoothly, cash begins to pour into the bucket. With each turn of the engine, a certain quantity of cash is produced. Turning the engine faster throws more cash into the bucket. You can also throw off more cash by making the engine bigger, or reducing the amount that is used in each cycle. Whatever route you choose (and it will probably be a combination of ways), your task as a business manager is pretty well defined: constantly look for ways to tune the engine to increase the cash that comes out of it.

The Task of the Sales Professional

Seen in this light, your customer's cash flow engine is really not that complicated. Your task is to find as many ways as possible to apply your products or services to improve its operation. Your success in this task (and your commission check) will be proportional to your understanding of the engine. There are five fundamental leverage points available to you to improve the engine, organized into three categories:

Efficiency

1. Reduce the amount taken out (lower costs).
2. Reduce the amount needed to run it (improve asset efficiency).

Effectiveness

3. Make it bigger (increase the volume running through it).
4. Make the buckets bigger (increase the gross profit margin).

Speed

5. Make it run faster.

Efficiency can be enhanced both by cutting costs and by improving the efficiency of assets. The first is the more common approach. The more you know about your customers' cost structures, the easier it will be to spot opportunities for reductions. There is also another, often overlooked, route to efficiency. Managers are trying to make their operations as lean as possible, squeezing as much productivity as they can out of each asset. You will learn to find ways for your customers to accomplish more with fewer assets.

Effectiveness concentrates on finding ways to improve your customers' revenues and gross profit margins and improving non–income statement measures of effectiveness such as customer satisfaction.

Speed focuses on ways to make the engine run faster. Because every revolution of the engine throws off cash, making it turn more times during the year will increase the cash thrown off. Every day spent in the business cycle costs the company a measurable amount, and shaving time from the cycle will return that cash to the bucket for more productive uses elsewhere. There are also some definite financial advantages to be gained by being first to market with new products.

The three categories of benefits are interrelated. Cost reductions may enable a company to lower prices and increase revenue through greater volume, for example. The benefit of understanding business improvements in this detailed manner is that you will not leave money on the table. Often salespeople concentrate on one class of benefits to the exclusion of others that are possible. Besides reducing the perceived value of their solutions, it limits the potential number of beneficiaries or problem owners within the corporation.

THE VALUE CHAIN

In his book *Competitive Advantage,* Professor Michael Porter explained the workings of a business enterprise using a now-classic model called the value chain.[1] Applying the value chain model to your customer's business operations is another way to gain insight into how the company adds value to its customers and possibly point out ways that you can use your product to help the company add more. It is similar to the cash flow engine in many respects, but it can bring a different perspective.

The value chain was so named because the enterprise receives inputs, performs a variety of activities that add value to them, and sells them to customers. To do this, there are two principal categories of business processes: primary activities and secondary activities. Primary activities are the activities concerned with physically creating the product or service and making it available for customers to purchase and use. Secondary activities support the primary activities and make them possible.

First, let us understand the definitions of the value chain components, as shown in Figure 7-6, and then we can see how we can use

1. Michael Porter, *Competitive Advantage*, Free Press, 1985.

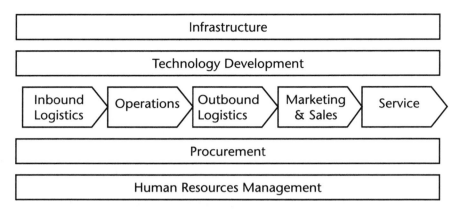

Figure 7-6. The Value Chain

the value chain model to help our customers improve their business operations.

Primary Activities

- *Inbound logistics* are the steps involved with receiving, storing, and distributing resources needed for the product.
- *Operations* are all the activities associated with transforming inputs into finished products.
- *Outbound logistics* are the steps needed to deliver the product or service to the customer.
- *Marketing and sales* must be done to make the product available to customers and induce them to buy.
- *Service* is all the activities that must be performed to keep buyers satisfied through installing, maintaining, or enhancing the product.

Secondary Activities

- *Infrastructure* includes general management, accounting and finance, planning, quality management, regulatory compliance, and others.
- *Technology development* refers to the activities dedicated to improving the product or processes.

- *Procurement* is the function of purchasing inputs for the various activities.
- *Human resources management* includes recruiting, hiring, training, testing, development, and compensation, plus all other activities associated with attracting and keeping people.

There is a temptation to think of secondary activities as "overhead," with the negative connotations associated with that term. However, secondary activities can add just as much value to the end customer as primary activities. For example, technology development ensures that the firm has a product that continues to appeal to the market, or even may create new markets. Even procurement can contribute directly to the bottom line, as Wal-Mart has proved.

The value chain provides a broad overview of the chain of activities in which your customer must engage to add value to its customers. Your solution will probably have an impact on one or more of the components. In those areas where you perceive you can add value, you must "drill down" to a greater level of detail and understand the dozens of steps and activities that your customers perform. That level of detail will help you to make a significant contribution, by opening up a wide range of possible ways that you can help them make the processes more effective, more efficient, or faster.

THE VALUE CHAIN AND THE CASH FLOW ENGINE

The cash flow engine and the value chain are very similar, because both are ways of describing reality. The primary activities of the value chain fit very well around the various stages in the cash flow engine, and the secondary activities all fit into the infrastructure component. Both are powerful in helping to clarify your customer's business operations and how they fit together to add value to the customers of that business. The cash flow engine is better at demonstrating the time component of business operations, which is one of the dimensions of value you can add to your customers, while the value chain provides more detail about the secondary activities.

ACTION POINTS

Now that you know how the basic cash flow engine and value chain work, there are two questions you need to think carefully about:

- How well do you know your customers' particular cash engines or value chains?
- What components does your product impact?

Because every company's cash flow engine or value chain is different, you must learn as much as possible about each customer's particular model, and the issues the company faces for each section.

For example, how much do you know about the components of the company's inventory? Does the business have excessive amounts of finished goods because of a problem with forecasting demand? How does the company's administrative burden compare with other companies in the industry? What are the issues the customer faces with regard to collecting its receivables?

Don't worry if you do not know too much right now. The important thing is to have a framework for learning more and asking better questions.

Now would be a good time to think about your product and the benefit it brings to your customers. Where do your benefits have an impact? Which parts of the cash flow engine does it affect? How can you help them increase their sales or earn a higher gross margin on the sales they make? Speed up their order-to-delivery cycle? Chapter 8, "Defining Your Product," will give you a useful framework to answer these questions.

Knowing the classes of business problems your product can solve gives you a head start in the search for particular sales opportunities. It will help you figure out whom to talk to and what questions to ask.

8

Defining Your Product

Before we turn to specific ways to help our customers improve their cash flow engines, the subject of the following chapters, we must take inventory of the tools available to apply to the task. These tools are the characteristics of your product and the benefits they bring to your customers. However, your total solution contains a package of benefits that is much bigger than just the product itself. You can increase the perceived value of your solution by defining it as broadly as possible.

THE OWNERSHIP EXPERIENCE

Most of us define our product in terms of what it does when it is being used for its intended purpose. A hammer pounds nails, gasoline powers engines, computers process data, a press prints documents. It's natural to think this way, because after all, that's what the products are designed to do.

However, from the customer's point of view, it is not that simple. The product impacts the customer in many more ways than in its daily operational use. The entire "ownership experience" includes the buying process, its daily use, and its maintenance and eventual replacement.

Think about the car you drive. There is much more to it than merely getting into a conveyance, turning the key, and traveling to your destination. Your entire experience of owning your car is encompassed by many aspects, like: shopping for the car, purchasing it, having a bewildering array of options, getting maintenance, fueling it, cleaning it, and knowing the resale value. In fact, some of the benefits you get you do not usually think about, such as safety and reliability. (Sometimes you don't think about what you are getting until you don't get it.)

Every aspect of the ownership experience affects your perception of the value of the car you own. And everybody else is affected differently. That's why there are so many different cars on the road.

The same applies to the product you sell. There is much more to the ownership experience than how the product is used operationally. And no two customers are alike in their perceptions of your product.

Your product is defined much more broadly than its features and the explicit functions it provides. The perceived value of your product is dependent on how well you can define all of its benefits that the customer will experience. The following methods to help you define your product more broadly will yield a surprising number of attributes that you have available to offer your customers, all of which can add up to significantly more value than the core product itself.

DEFINING THE PRODUCT

There are several ways to look at the product you sell:

- The total product concept
- The life cycle concept
- Its impact on the customer's cash flow engine

Of these, the first two are established models in marketing thought. The third model is one you learned in the last chapter. Each is valuable by itself, but putting the three together creates a powerful method to think about your product and to present the total solution to the customer. In other words, you must decide what you are really selling and what your customers think they are buying.

Let's take a look at each model and use it to expand our definition of the product we sell. In doing so, we will be building a new combined model which will help us discover and present every possible dollar of value we have to offer each of our customers.

The Total Product

At the most basic level, we can think of our product (whether tangible or intangible) as a box containing a number of features and corresponding benefits:

The features and benefits contained in the box are apparent to all customers and have a defined value in the market. An automobile, for instance, seats a specific number of passengers and has a known top speed and mileage characteristics.

But there is more to the product than the box contains. The first thing we need to do is examine the total product. In *The Marketing Imagination* (Free Press, 1983), Theodore Levitt defined the total product as comprising four zones:

1. The generic product
2. The expected product
3. The augmented product
4. The potential product

The *generic product* is the thing being sold, which is represented by the box in Figure 8-1.

The *expected product* represents the minimum characteristics and performance the customer expects. Performance characteristics can be separate from the product itself: purchase convenience, payment terms, timeliness of delivery, after-sale support, and so on. It might include commonly expected delivery and payment terms, and even such factors as safety and convenience. For a fast-food restaurant, the generic product is the food, and the safety of the parking lot and the cleanliness of the rest rooms would be part of the expected product. For a software vendor, technical support would be an essential part.

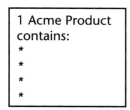

Figure 8-1. Product Basics

Staying with the car example, the expected product includes bank financing, a warranty, and a reasonably close dealership. The market will ruthlessly set the parameters of the expected product; a dealer who does not offer these minimum features will not last long in a competitive market.

It is the responsibility of the company's management, marketing, and manufacturing to provide the generic and expected product. This is the bare minimum the salesperson needs to be able to play in the game. As a salesperson, you do not have to do too much to provide these to your customer. (Although, if the competition has not met the minimum conditions, it would be fair game to point that out to your prospect.) However, if that were all that were needed, the most prized sales skill would be the ability to process orders efficiently. The next two areas are where superior selling skills can make a difference.

The *augmented product* is everything that you offer that exceeds the customer's minimum expectations, as long as those characteristics add value to the customer. (It is possible to offer more than the customer expects without adding value; if your product is higher-quality than customers need, they will certainly not see a reason for paying more for it.) It could be performance characteristics of the product itself that exceed the customer's expectations, but these will not have value to the customer unless the customer understands how the additional performance can help the company. You may offer additional value that is not connected to the physical product, such as better training in the use of the product or superior support after the sale. The augmented facet of the product is a function of the attributes of the product plus your ability to influence the customer's perception of their value. It's not a better mousetrap that brings the world to your door; it's your skill in demonstrating the value of the new mousetrap. This is where competing offerings are differentiated, value is defined, and sales are won or lost.

The *potential product* is everything that the product could be for your customer, sometimes through the application of new technology, but more frequently through greater imagination in your quest for new ways to add value.

In Figure 8-2, the gray zone exists just as much in the customer's mind as in the attributes of the product. It is your job to expand the gray zone as much as possible. You can best accomplish this through

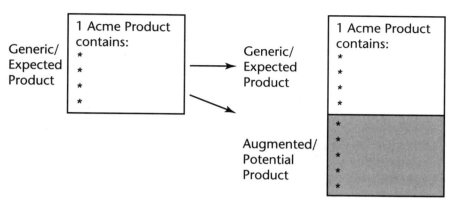

Figure 8-2. Expanding the Product

a careful examination of the benefits you can deliver at all stages of the product life cycle.

The Product Life Cycle

Another way to extend the definition of your product is to look at the ownership experience over time. Your product does not begin providing benefits to your customers the instant they decide they need it; even with the simplest of products, there is some time, effort, and cost involved in putting the product into position to begin delivering its benefits. As products grow in complexity, these factors may be the most critical part of the entire ownership experience. On the other end of the time scale, it's unrealistic to expect the product to deliver its benefits without occasional problems or to work forever. It will often require maintenance and will eventually need to be upgraded or replaced.

To account for these factors, we must expand the definition of the product to include the critical phases of its ownership experience before and after the "operational" phase. Every complex sale includes a "Get-it, Use-it, and Fix-it" phase, which is shown in Figure 8-3.[1]

---

1. A useful description of the thought process can be found in *Customer Intimacy, Knowledge Exchange,* 1996, by Fred Wiersema.

	Implementation	Operational	Support/Growth
Generic/ Expected Product	1 Acme Product contains: * * * *	1 Acme Product contains: * * * *	1 Acme Product contains: * * * *
Augmented/ Potential Product	* * * * *	* * * * *	* * * * *

Figure 8-3.   Three Life Cycle Stages

Picturing this thought process, we see that our product box has now expanded horizontally to include the entire product life cycle. The original product box is the operational phase, and depending on the product, it is not always the most important. The implementation phase is critical to delivering the product into an operational capability, and the support and growth phase will help ensure that its benefits are continued and enhanced.

Implementation covers all the activities that must take place between the time the customer first feels a need for change and the time the product is operational, delivering the promised benefits. With complex systems, this phase can last several years and encompass such activities as specifying requirements, researching and evaluating options, designing possible solutions, testing, ordering, delivering, installing, trouble-shooting, and so on. As products grow in complexity, this phase becomes the most critical. There are two reasons for this. First, risk is highest in this phase because the customer (and often the salesperson) is not certain the product will work as advertised. Second, many of the activities of this phase affect the level and quality of results that are finally delivered in the operational phase.

Operation covers the daily use of the product once it begins delivering results, until the first time it needs maintenance or upgrade. It includes all the characteristics that influence how well the product works and the benefits it delivers.

Support/Growth covers all the activities that maintain and grow the benefits provided during the operational phase, including technical support, user help, preventive maintenance, repairs, upgrades, and replacement. It is often the crucial phase in determining the difference between one-time transactions and enduring customer relationships.

Impact on the Cash Flow Engine

There is one more thought process that we need to add to our model before it is complete. Everything that our total product does for the customer during each of its life cycle phases must be considered in terms of the impact it has on the customer's cash flow engine. That is the only way to build a bridge between our product's performance and measurable financial benefits. Unless a specific attribute of your product can have a positive impact on your customer's business operations, it adds no value and is irrelevant to the selling process.

To make the thought process easier, we now extend the definition of the product, resulting in the Total Solution Table depicted in Figure 8-4.

In the implementation phase, a number of differentiators will affect the speed and reliability with which the product is implemented in the customer's operations. The most obvious is speed. Once the customer is convinced that the product will deliver measurable benefits, the primary concerns become:

- How quickly can we get it in place?
- How sure are we that it will deliver the promised benefits?

If the customer expects a tangible financial return from using the product, every day lost in implementation costs the customer money, so speed of implementation becomes critical. Speed is affected by many factors, including delivery dates, time to install or customize, and response time to customer requests. Sometimes the customer is willing to pay more for "good enough" delivered immediately than for the "best" delivered later, especially in today's fast-paced business environment. On the other hand, if you are sup-

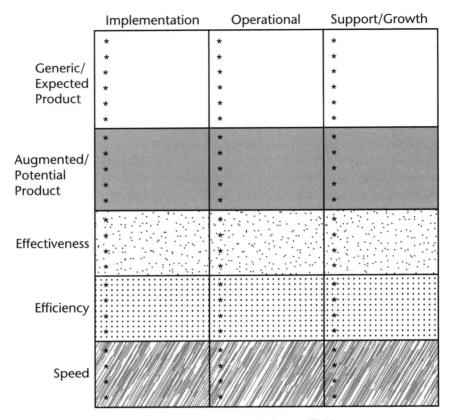

Figure 8-4.   The Total Solution Table

plying a critical component of the space shuttle, speed is a distant second to reliability.

Using speed as an example, perhaps faster implementation of your system can be linked to shortening the customer's time to market of a new product, which can affect all three aspects of your customer's cash flow engine:

- Effectiveness: the sooner the product is on the market, the sooner revenues begin flowing in.
- Efficiency: time saved in product development means money saved.

• Speed: market leaders can often command higher profit margins and can carve out higher market share.

Getting your customer to think about your solution in these terms can make operational issues such as minor performance differences and costs seem insignificant in comparison.

Listed here are some of the most common factors to think about in the implementation phase:

• Training
• User friendliness
• Conversion costs
• Speed of delivery
• Response to requests
• Customization

• Flexibility
• Payment terms
• Purchase sizes
• Packaging
• Implementation plan
• Compatibility with existing system

Advantages during the support and growth phase relate to the following:

• Mean time between failures
• Repair time
• Response time
• Guarantees
• Service costs
• Locations
• Repair convenience

• On-line support
• Trade-in value
• Market for used equipment
• Consulting services
• Ease of upgrades
• Interoperability

These lists are generic. You should take the time now to create your own matrix of differentiators across the entire life cycle of your product.

USING THE TOTAL SOLUTION TABLE

To use the Total Solution Table effectively, you must first take inventory of all the attributes of your solution across its entire life cycle. Pay special attention to the augmented product, because that is where answers are less obvious and might require imagination. Once you have come up with a list of potential differentiators, there are three steps:

1. Narrow down the list to the attributes in which you think you can demonstrate an advantage. It is highly unlikely that your solution will be better or worse across the board.
2. Get agreement from your customer that you have an advantage. It's not an advantage until the customer agrees that it is. Every customer is attracted by different things about a product.
3. Quantify the value of the advantage using the cash flow engine as a model. For this step you will have to get agreement from your customer on the profit or cash flow improvement afforded by each feature. The following three chapters show how to do this.

Here's an example:

A maker of components for engines uses electronic data interchange (EDI) to provide continuous replenishment to the assembler. The assembler saves money by eliminating the need to keep inventory on hand and by reducing the number of times the assembly line goes down due to a lack of parts. (*Speed* and *Efficiency*) The assembler in turn is able to promise its own customers rapid turnaround time on custom orders, thus allowing higher profit margins. (*Effectiveness*)

From this example you can see how a product that might otherwise be indistinguishable from its competitor can be shown to have much more value because of an advantage in the implementation phase. Continue the process across the product's life cycle: fill in your strengths, and then tie each to its effect on your customer's business operations. Your completed table will look similar to Figure 8-5.

As you do the exercise, a few snags may develop. First, you may not know enough about your customer or your own product to fill the table out completely. This is not so bad, because the results will quickly bring out the weaknesses in your sales effort and point you in the direction you need to go. Second, you will probably find areas where your competitor has quantifiable advantages. This is not so bad either, because it will prepare you for potential objections. Obviously, it's not your responsibility to bring those up, but the Total Solution Table can help you prepare for them.

	Implementation	Operational	Support/Growth
Generic/ Expected Product	* training * * * *	* higher quality * * * *	* * * * *
Augmented/ Potential Product	* EDI– continuous replenishment * * *	* * * * *	* * * * *
Effectiveness	* faster custom orders—higher profit margins ($250,000) * customer satisfaction * * *	* fewer returns— greater customer satisfaction * fewer rejections— higher production *	* * * * * * * *
Efficiency	* reduce parts inventory ($100,000) * fewer invoices ($5,000) * less downtime ($200,000) *	* reduce inspection costs ($50,000) * * * * *	* * * * * * *
Speed	* faster changeovers * * * *	* * * * *	* * * * *
Total Value	$555,000	$50,000	

Figure 8-5. Completing the Total Solution Table

The table can be used in several ways:

- As a planning tool—Use it to gain a thorough understanding and clarify your own thinking about the attributes of your solutions and their potential value. Perhaps the best way to do this is to create a generic table, with the help of the sales team, for each product you offer. Then, use that one as a template to plan your approach to individual customers.
- As a presentation tool—Complex systems have so many different attributes that it can be very difficult to clearly state your case to your customer, just as it can be very confusing to the customer to listen to several different claims. The clearest solutions are the most compelling, and the Total Solution Table can be used to crisply focus on the real issues.

ACTION POINTS

Get together with other members of the sales team, including sales management, sales support, technical support, and marketing, and develop one or more Total Solution Tables. Do them by product and by customer type (e.g., specific industry). If you are not able to complete one on the first try, this will point out the information you need to build a compelling business case for your customer.

9

Efficiency

To begin our quest for measurable business improvements for our customers, we are going to look for ways to depress the operating-cost line of the company's profit wedge by making their business operations more efficient. For a working definition of *efficiency*, let's revisit the productivity equation we first looked at in Chapter 2:

$$\text{Productivity} = \frac{\text{Output}}{\text{Input}} \times \text{Speed}$$

Our concern with improving our customers' business efficiency is to find ways to help them reduce the inputs required to achieve a given level of output. The efficiency focus is internal, as opposed to effectiveness which is much more focused on the corporation's external transactions. Of course, it is important to remember that internal improvements can easily translate into external results, as when a company succeeds in becoming the low-cost producer in its peer group and uses lower pricing to seize market share.

In the language of the cash flow engine, efficiency is concerned with two goals. Our first concern is to help our customers reduce the leakage from the system, and the second is to help them obtain more output from the company's existing asset base. In other words, we will show them how to reduce costs and increase their asset efficiency.

WHY YOU NEED TO KNOW THIS

Although this book has continually stressed the need to look beyond cost savings in order to demonstrate the value that your product brings to your customer, the search for efficiencies is still the "500-pound gorilla" in your customers' minds. While business managers today are focusing greater attention on increasing revenues and on qualitative improvements, they have by no means given up on finding ways to cut costs. As if you haven't heard it enough, business is extremely competitive nowadays—so competitive, in fact, that the traditional trade-off between price and quality is becoming obsolete. Your customers' customers increasingly want to have their cake and eat it too, demanding top quality and state-of-the-art performance, all at low prices. Quite simply, low costs are the admission price that today's companies pay to play the game. And the price is always getting tougher to pay. In order to compete, companies will of course have to differentiate themselves and add value to their customers, but they will always have to do it at an acceptable price. The pressure to contain costs will not go away, even if all the other pressures piled on top of it obscure it.

Contributing to these pressures is the performance of the economy during the last decade. When double-digit inflation was perceived as a fact of life, it was easier to pass on price increases to customers, who expected it and could in turn pass on the increases to their customers. Inflation is an almost negligible factor today, making price increases much more difficult to justify.

Your customers' pricing pressures, therefore, are as heavy as they have ever been, so most if not all of your buyers will always be interested in saving money. It is critical to know exactly how your product or service will help them do it.

In addition, if you understand the true causes of waste and inefficiency, you might be able to spot hidden opportunities to help your customers. This has a triple effect: your customers will see you as a true problem solver who adds value to the sales process, you will increase the value of your solution, and you will find opportunities that your competitors might miss.

FINDING EFFICIENCIES

Your sales or problem-solving process in helping a customer cut costs is relatively straightforward: you must first understand the company's cost structure, which is a reflection of the various business processes it employs; identify the business processes that you can impact with your product; and demonstrate and quantify the benefit you bring to the right people.

There are five general paths you can follow to bring efficiency improvements to your customers:

1. Lower the price they pay for your product.
2. Reduce the comparative cost of ownership for your product.
3. Avoid future costs.
4. Make their business processes more efficient by reducing waste.
5. Help them make more efficient use of their assets.

Let's review each.

Lowering the Price

Sometimes you have to resort to markdowns, but you don't need this book to tell you how to do that. That's not selling; it's accounting.

Lowering the Total Cost of Ownership

In many of the sales situations you face, the target customer has already decided to buy the product or service you sell but has not yet chosen a vendor. The company puts the project out to bid, or simply plays you off against the other competitors, hoping to use the competitive process to extract the lowest possible price out of the market. Unfortunately salespeople often make the mistake of taking customers too literally. It is not your job to simply provide the lowest price: it is your responsibility to demonstrate the best cost.

The key word in that last sentence is *cost*. Too many people equate price with cost, when in fact there may be little correlation between the two. *Price* refers to the actual invoiced charge that your customer will pay to acquire your product. It is only one of the components of total cost. Cost includes the price paid but also far more. It includes all of the expenditures of money, time, and effort required to realize maximum benefit out of the product. For example, analysts estimate that the price of the typical desktop computer in the corporate environment is only about 5 percent of the actual lifetime cost involved.

The bulk of the cost of ownership comes from installing and maintaining software, dealing with problems, learning how to use the features, downtime, and similar factors.

While price is paid once, cost may be paid throughout the entire life of the product, even before the product is selected. Frequently the lowest-priced product in the mix turns out to be the highest-cost selection. For example, suppose your equipment costs 20 percent more than the competitor's but your price includes detailed implementation assistance and training which allows your customer to begin using your system effectively several weeks earlier. If that product can help the customer save money, or make more money, then the money lost by not using your product should be added to your competitor's price to arrive at the total cost. Similarly, more rugged products that carry a higher price tag but last longer may have a far lower life-cycle cost. You must consider not only the future replacement cost of the item but also the additional downtime, lost revenue, hassle, and so on of going through the replacement process.

Price is a factor to which everyone pays attention mainly because it is the most visible. When things are easily seen, it is natural that more attention is paid to them than is logically warranted. If your competitor has a lower price than you offer, don't expect the company to bring up the differences that would make its cost of ownership higher! In fact, while price is highly visible, most purchases include hidden costs which sometimes need to be brought to the attention of the decision maker. Hidden costs include:

- Transaction costs—These may include the actual dollar costs involved with getting the product delivered and installed, plus time and effort expended by the buyer in selecting and taking delivery of the product.
- Opportunity costs—The buyers must be made aware of what they are giving up in order to gain the benefits from the product, as the dollars, time, and effort could have been used for something else.
- Maintenance costs—The costs associated with keeping the product running at capacity and keeping users happy.
- Accommodation costs—This term refers to the costs associated with disrupting established routines in order to make the product work. For example, is there downtime while the product is

installed, or do things need to be moved, or are other processes adversely affected? How well will it work while users are getting accustomed to a different way of doing things?

This discussion may seem very basic, but it needs constant reminding. We all fall too easily into the trap of comparing prices when we should be comparing costs. If we want to ensure that our customers focus on the life-cycle costs, we must first prepare ourselves to think in these terms. The best tool for preparation and presentation of the total life-cycle costs is the Total Solution Table that is introduced in Chapter 8. Once we are prepared, we can ensure that all issues relevant to the total cost of the solution are brought out.

It is ironic that buyers can sometimes be their own worst enemies when it comes to seeking out the lowest price. As we have seen, sometimes the excessive focus on price can blind them to factors that will drive up their total costs in the long run. Frequently the greatest cost of an excessive focus on price is the benefit forgone during the time it takes to search out the lowest price. Keep in mind that corporate investments are made with a goal of realizing a return on the investment. The money is spent because some benefit accrues to the purchaser. However, that benefit cannot be realized until the system is purchased and installed. Time lost in seeking out the lowest price through an extensive and complex bidding process frequently carries a much greater cost than the small price difference gained. Although not as visible, opportunity costs are just as real as if checks were written.

Avoiding Future Costs

Do you remember the old commercial where the pitchman said: "You can pay me now—or pay me later"? That is the whole idea of cost avoidance. Sometimes your customers need to spend money today to avoid spending money in the future. The most obvious application of this idea is an insurance policy, but many of the products we sell have at least some element of an insurance policy built in. For example, you may sell a product that gives customer service agents the ability to handle more complaints in the same time. This will avoid the need to hire additional agents as business grows. Maintenance agreements and service plans are another form of insurance policy. Expenditures to avoid breakdowns or to protect existing assets are also common examples.

Making Business Processes More Efficient

Now we turn to the real art and practice of becoming a consultant to your customers: combining your product expertise with an intimate knowledge of their business processes in order to make them more efficient. First we will look at how to improve your understanding of your customers' true costs.

Understanding Your Customer's Cost Structure

You can't help your customers reduce their costs until you clearly understand what those costs are. There are two keys to understanding your customer's cost structure: line-item expenses and process costs. Knowing your customer's line-item expenses will help you diagnose potential areas for improvement, but knowing their process costs is the most effective way to prescribe workable solutions.

Line-Item Expenses

Line-item expenses are the expense categories that show up on the income statement. Generally speaking, they cover the entire range of the company's activities and expenditures in broad categories. Examples of line-item categories are selling expenses, financing charges, and labor costs of manufacturing. We are already familiar with the broad categories from the financial statement module (Chapter 4), although it is sometimes possible to find finer-grained information on specific departments or activities from your clients.

The line-item approach to understanding your customer's cost structure has a number of advantages, the principal one being that it is generally easy to obtain the information you need, at least in the broad brush strokes of the financial statement. In addition, because the information is presented in a standardized format, it is relatively simple to compare your customer with similar companies. This is useful in spotting potential problem areas for further examination.

The standardized format also makes it a snap to spot potential trends by analyzing changes in expenditures over time.

The ability to compare costs with other companies or with past performance will not give you the answers you need, but it will provide clues for further research and questioning. (The clues also become easier to discover as you gain experience with companies in a particular industry.) The improved quality of your questions as a result of a solid base of information should make your initial sales calls much more effective. In fact, this level of knowledge will be indispensable in earning the right to talk to higher-level decision makers in the first place.

Within the advantages of the line-item approach can also be found its weaknesses. The broad nature of the numbers does not contain the detail you need, except in a general sense, to diagnose specific problems. While the information can help you detect that there is a problem or an opportunity for improvement, it might not help you determine exactly what the problem is.

Another limitation of the line-item approach is that the numbers usually cut across the entire company. Unless you are already positioned at the highest levels of the company in your sales process, the people to whom you are talking are not going to be specifically concerned with the broad numbers. They are measured in finer detail, and you will have to get to that level. In the same vein, when is the last time you called on the "Vice President of Selling, General, and Administrative Expenses"? The people to whom you sell have concerns that cut across the expense categories.

Finally, always keep in mind that the line-item numbers you see on your customer's financial statement are historical information. By the time you see them, the numbers reflect performance that is at least several months old. Just as you would not drive a car by looking in the rearview mirror and trying to anticipate upcoming road conditions, you cannot rely only on historical financial information to make predictions about the effect of your solution on your customer's business.

Because of these limitations, line-item analysis of your customers' costs should not be your only approach. However, it is an excellent starting point for diagnosing their earnings challenges. Finding the cure, however, will generally require knowledge of their process or activity costs.

Advantages of the Process Approach

The process approach supplements the line-item approach in several ways. First, it makes the connection between the numbers and the processes clearer, which can simplify your task of diagnosing problems and prescribing solutions. It will be easier for you to find ways to cut your customers' costs if you keep in mind that high costs are merely symptoms of an underlying problem; they indicate that something is amiss in the process. Your job is to understand the processes and search for the underlying causes of high costs, because eliminating or otherwise influencing those causes is the only way to make a measurable impact on costs. You don't lower your customer's costs; you solve the problem or eliminate the cause of the high cost. Never forget that the numbers on your customer's income statement are not reality. They are representations of reality based on generally accepted accounting principles. They merely reflect measurements of the results of the company's many and varied business activities. You must first know the effect your solution has on these activities, and the numbers will take care of themselves.

Second, the process approach can make the impact of your solution more immediate. Performance improvements predict financial improvements. Physical performance changes can be seen immediately; the financial results may not show up until the quarterly income statement.

Finally, the most practical benefit of the process approach is that the decision makers to whom you are selling are generally more aware of their process challenges on a daily basis than of their income statements.

Input Reduction

Every business is a collection of people engaged in many tasks and activities, and activities that are governed by a common goal are called *processes*. Every process is a managed collection of inputs—including labor, capital, time, expertise, and space—designed to yield a specific output. The numbers you see reported are measurements of the costs and effects of those processes. The only way to truly understand the business, and help the business to improve, is to gain a thorough understanding of the underlying processes. You must know:

1. What are the inputs used in your customer's processes, and why?
2. What can you do to help the company reduce inputs?
3. How will you measure the results?

Understanding Inputs and Their Reasons

The value chain approach discussed in Chapter 7 is a useful way of getting an overview of your customers' business processes. First determine which processes you can affect, and then try to answer the process-improvement questions just listed, focusing on potential reductions in three areas: methods, materials, and people.

Methods are the steps involved in the process and the effects of those steps. The activities in methods take time and produce specific results. Some methods exist because that is the way it has always been done, or because no one has thought of a better way, or because constraints exist. Many of these constraints—of capacity, distance, speed—are grounded in the technologies used.

Many processes require materials. Sometimes the material is as obvious as waste metal produced in manufacturing; other times it might require imagination, as in creating a different design to use less material.

Finally, processes contain people costs. How many people are needed to run the process? How much output is possible per person under the current methods, and how much is possible using your product? If you demonstrate that a process can be conducted with fewer people, make sure that you deduct their fully burdened cost. The cost of keeping an employee is often far greater than the person's nominal salary. It includes benefits, additional taxes paid on the employee's behalf, and other indirect expenses such as office space and other amenities.

It's also important to take into account the effects a specific process has on other processes in the corporation. It does no good to reduce costs from one process if the outputs produce higher costs in another process. Frequently processes are made deliberately expensive in order to provide better inputs down the line.

Getting Rid of Waste

Perhaps the best way to think about efficiency improvements is in terms of reducing or eliminating waste. Every process contains an enormous amount of waste. Waste is more than unneeded materials left over after a job is completed. In this context, it is defined as any activity that uses resources but does not add value to the product. Value, of course, is defined by your customer's customer.

Such a tight definition of waste opens up a very large range of opportunity for reducing or eliminating waste in most business processes. Lean manufacturing techniques developed by Japanese companies brought to light many commonplace examples of business processes in which less than 2 percent of the time spent and very little of the money was actually used in adding value to the end customer. Some of these opportunities are obvious, and some require a little more searching.

For example, consider your own sales process. Part of your time, of course, is spent in front of customers, discovering and demonstrating ways in which to improve their business processes, helping them implement your solution, or showing them how to get maximum benefit out of your product. These activities add value to your customers.

On the other hand, take a minute to think about all the other things your job requires: filling out call reports and expense reports, tracking down information for your customers and your bosses, attending meetings, traveling to customer sites, looking up or adding to customer information, solving problems for customers because an order was not received when promised. None of these activities adds value to your customers.

This is not to say they should not be done. We will never get away entirely from pesky administrative requirements, because the information is necessary to ensure the "smooth" functioning of the corporation. However, recent history is full of cases of process improvements. For example, many sales force automation projects attempt to slash these sources of waste by eliminating double entry of information, thus making repeated trips back and forth to get information unnecessary, and getting rid of errors that can crop up whenever information is transcribed.

It can be easier to catch waste in a process if you keep an eye out for the various ways waste can creep in:

- Mistakes can occur that require rectification. Sometimes the cost of fixing mistakes ripples throughout various processes, as when products are recalled, and can have consequences beyond the immediate cost of fixing them, such as customer dissatisfaction and lost business.

- The process may produce items that nobody wants. One common example is reports that are generated long after the need for the information has vanished.
- Some of the processing steps may not be needed. Perhaps you can provide a part that does not need to be reworked, for example.
- Movement of employees may occur without purpose. Think about this one the next time you attend one of your sales meetings to receive information that could have been distributed via E-mail or a conference call.
- Transport of goods may occur without purpose. As you will see in the discussion in Chapter 11 on speed improvements, many manufacturing processes are set up with all the same types of machinery in one area, necessitating frequent movement of the goods being processed.
- People or assets may be waiting idle because an upstream activity has not been completed.
- Goods and services may not meet the needs of the customer. For example, I have never been able to figure out why some cars require separate keys for the ignition and the trunk. Or, what percentage of the features of your most common software applications do you use?
- One of the most common reasons for waste creeping into a process is the inability to measure all the costs and inputs of that process. Perhaps your solution can help your customer get a better handle on costs; you may be able to provide that ability through your experience in working with the same process for similar customers.

While this analysis might help you find plenty of opportunities for slashing costs from your customers' processes, it represents the potential for improvement only of a single process. When you look at the many processes, you will find that there exist many other opportunities for reducing waste by improving the *linkages* between them. If you can improve the output from one process, it may make another downstream process easier, faster, or cheaper to perform. Simple examples include convenient packaging and quality materials that fit right the first time.

How Do You Do It?

On the face of it, this may seem a little presumptuous. How can you, an outsider, possibly improve your customers' processes, if they represent the best thinking of the people who are intimately involved with those processes day to day?

In fact, however, there may be dozens of opportunities in every business process for reducing costs, efforts, time, or materials. Virtually any business operation can be improved upon, with the application of a little more thought, imagination, discipline, or technology. Any company worth its salt has long ago implemented a constant-improvement program and has found that today's processes, which represent the best ideas of those who understand them best, somehow can always be improved tomorrow.

Sometimes the perspective of an outsider is just what is needed to discern fresh opportunities. If you have a sales concentration in a particular industry, you frequently have the advantage of seeing many different approaches to the same problems. To the extent that you do not violate confidentiality, this experience may be welcomed by many of your prospects.

Finally, many process improvements are merely waiting for new enabling technologies to make them happen. Frequently your customers know exactly what they would like but are not immediately aware when the solution arrives on the market. For example, many companies involved in field-service dispatch recognize the benefits of wireless data communications to enable their service personnel to access vital customer information while on the road, but the technology to do that reliably, simply, and inexpensively is only just beginning to reach the market.

How Do You Apply This?

Being able to use the process approach in your sales efforts requires research and planning. The research consists of several functions.

First you must thoroughly understand your customers' cost structure, from both the line-item and the process perspectives. This requires that you do the research as specified in Chapter 6, reading their annual reports, reading analysts' reports, understanding their industries, and even reading their competitors' annuals. While this may seem like a lot of work, console yourself with the thought that it will make a tremendous difference in the way you appear to your prospects.

You must know not only the numbers but also the reasons for those numbers. Keep in mind that different cost structures may reflect conscious trade-offs by your customer to differentiate itself from competitors, so don't assume automatically that higher costs in one area mean that your customer has problems that must be corrected. A gourmet restaurant is going to have much higher service costs than a fast-food establishment; you can't go in there and promise to make them as efficient as McDonald's.

With this understanding, you will want to spend some time thinking about your product and listing all the various business processes that you can impact. Note that this might not be an individual effort. In fact, it may be a strategic initiative to be undertaken by your entire sales management, with assistance from marketing and even your financial people.

Second, go back to your existing customers and gather information and testimonials regarding the benefits your product has brought them. The more detail you can get, especially hard numbers, the better off you are. Be sure that you have a clear understanding of which information you have permission to use, and how much detail you can divulge, in your selling efforts.

Finally, be sure you consider who in your target organization would be most responsible for the processes you have targeted for improvement. These are the people who will be most willing to listen to your ideas.

Asset Efficiency

Unlike cost reduction, which affects only your customer's income statement, asset efficiency affects the relationship between the balance sheet and the income statement. This fifth and final path to improving efficiency relates revenues and income to the level of investment needed to achieve it.

Asset efficiency is becoming a more fertile ground to search for business-improvement opportunities for your customers, as the relentless pursuit of improvement by companies is forcing managers to make do with less. It is showing up in the concerns of top managers, as the AlliedSignal 1992 annual report indicates:

> . . . our ambition is to increase [working capital] turns to 5.2 by 1994. This one full turn improvement will free up about $500 million in cash, which will provide ample resources to fund our growth opportunities.

We often overlook asset-efficiency improvements when demonstrating the value that we can bring to our customers. Part of the reason is that improvements in this area, paradoxically, may not result in profit increases to our customers, even though they can be of tremendous benefit to the balance sheet.

The explanation for this is found in the differentiation between profits and cash flow. Suppose you implement a system for your customer that allows the company to produce the same amount of widgets as before but frees up one widget machine which can then be sold. If that widget machine is sold for book value, the net effect on profitability will be zero. In an accounting sense, you have not helped your customery make any money. On the other hand, the cash generated from the sale of the widget machine is real and may be used for other productive investments. So, while profits are not affected, cash flow is definitely helped.

Any improvements in asset efficiency for your customers may be applied in one of two ways: either the company continues at a given revenue level, thus throwing off cash which can be used for other purposes, or additional revenue is possible without additional cash investment.

Asset Efficiency and the Cash Flow Engine

Looking back at our cash flow engine model of the business, we see that cash tends to accumulate in four principal areas:

- Cash
- Accounts receivable
- Inventory
- Fixed assets

Obviously a certain amount of cash is needed to keep the engine running smoothly, just like oil in your car's engine. However, most firms have more cash tied up in these categories than is absolutely essential. One of the greatest opportunities of focusing on this area is that often your solution may free up more cash from your customer's business operations than the solution will actually cost them.

Reducing Operating Assets

A firm's financial managers walk a daily tightrope, trying to ensure that they have the correct amount of assets on the books. Assets on the books can almost be thought of as liabilities, because they tie up cash, so the ideal situation would be to operate with only the exact assets needed at that particular moment. Managers, ideally, are always striving to reduce their company's investment in assets. On the other hand, a certain level of assets in various categories is inevitable and necessary to ensure smooth functioning of operations.

When customers want to buy, inventory must be available to fulfill the order without undue delay. Many customers purchase on credit, so a certain amount of accounts receivable is inevitable, and the company must of course have cash in its accounts to pay daily obligations and to cover checks as they clear. At the same time, it probably owns property housing its offices and operations, and equipment to manufacture or generate its product.

The balancing act is this: too much invested in assets means that the company is not running as efficiently as it could and is "leaving money on the table"; too little invested in assets, and the company might not be able to operate smoothly. It's like a football player: if he is too fat, he might not be able to move quickly enough to make plays, but if he is too light, he will get pushed around too easily.

Remember: an asset is only an asset if it is used productively. Otherwise it is a liability.

Figure 9-1 summarizes the consequences of letting operating assets get out of balance.

Reducing Inventory

Inventory is probably the most promising area of the three operating assets listed for finding ways to help your customer save money and free up cash. The well-publicized focus on just-in-time inventory pro-

	Too Low	OK	Too High
Cash	• Missed payments • Can't buy supplies or inventory • Management distraction • Lost opportunities • Bankruptcy		• Missed investment opportunities • Low returns
Inventory	• Slow turnaround • Unfilled orders • Dissatisfied customers • Peak-period inefficiency • Lost sales from stockouts		• Not enough cash • High financing costs • Obsolescence • Damage • Wrong mix • Takes up space • Lose touch with market • Markdowns
Accounts Receivable	• Lost sales • Customer dissatisfaction		• Not enough cash • Customer unhappiness with collection efforts • High financing costs • Bad-debt losses

Figure 9-1. Effects of Imbalance in Operating Assets

cesses attests to the importance attached to proper inventory management among business leaders. Anything you can do to help your customers operate smoothly with lower levels of inventory on hand is bound to generate interest.

Everybody talks about reducing inventory, but it can be very difficult to actually do anything about it. The tricky part about inventory is that you need so much of it on hand in order to meet any of the countless needs expressed by unpredictable customers. You need enough in the pipeline just to meet normal demand, plus a cushion to handle unexpected surges; you need to have enough variety on hand to accommodate shifting taste; even obsolete parts may have to be stocked to take care of customers who refuse to buy your latest and greatest model. If anything, the problem is becoming even more acute as customers demand "mass customization," driving up the varieties needed just to placate an increasingly finicky customer base.

Inventory management is a complex science/art that is beyond the scope of this book. The following list can give you a sense of some of the more common factors that must be taken into account. Use it as a checklist to help you diagnose some of the challenges faced by your customers, or as a starting point for further questioning.

- Difficulty in forecasting demand necessitates safety stocks
- Changing customer needs or tastes require large variety
- Changing customer needs or tastes cause obsolescence
- Long lead times and inflexible scheduling result in long production runs
- Improper scheduling results in idle time
- Poor quality process requires extensive reworking
- Long processing/manufacturing time
- Slow/inadequate communication from sales and marketing
- Large number of parts required for complex product lines
- Unreliable materials shipments from suppliers necessitate safety stocks
- Supplier incentives/pricings encourage larger orders
- Slow order-processing procedures
- Inflexibility in meeting special requests from customers
- Maintenance problems with equipment create idle time
- Product testing takes time
- New products/designs result in long learning curves
- Long lead time required to retool/retrain for new designs
- Poor inventory monitoring or tracking causes "lost" inventory

Fixed Assets

In many companies, fixed assets represent the vast majority of their investments: buildings to house factories and offices, vehicles, factory equipment, computers, telephone systems and office equipment, and so on. While it may be difficult to get rid of some of these, you may be able to help the company grow without incurring significant additions to its existing assets. To help your customer squeeze more efficiency out of fixed assets, consider these general approaches:

- Replace expensive assets with cheaper assets that do the same thing.
- Reduce bottlenecks through the system that limit the use of the asset.
- Make it easier to find the asset.
- Make the asset unnecessary.
- Reduce downtime through improved maintenance, reliability, and changeover time.
- Improve the performance of the asset.

Let's take a look at some examples. It may seem funny that your customer might need help finding their assets, but what if your customer is a transportation company, trying to extract maximum use out of its thousands of vehicles? The company makes money only when the vehicles are full and moving. Automatic vehicle location (AVL) systems are being implemented which keep track of vehicles, making it easier to find the nearest one to respond to requests, and allowing transportation companies to sell up to one-third of their fleets and still maintain customer service levels.

Another example: making the asset unnecessary. Arming mobile sales professionals with laptops and enabling them to access the company database from remote locations has allowed many companies to create virtual offices for their sales force. The advantage, of course, is that some of their rent payments can be made virtual as well.

Another way to make assets unnecessary has become very popular in recent years: outsourcing. Firms are focusing their efforts where their principal expertise gives them a competitive advantage and turning over noncore functions to outside companies. If you are providing an outsourcing service, you may not always be able to demonstrate lower expenditures on that particular function, but you may still be able to add value by reducing fixed-asset investment, thus improving your customer's cash position.

The lists presented in this section are not meant to be exhaustive. Your best bet is to do some planning, perhaps in conjunction with your marketing and finance people, to help you anticipate the asset-efficiency improvements you can make possible for your customers, determine who within your customer organizations would benefit the most from your solution, and then approach them with your value proposition built around asset efficiency.

ACTION POINTS

As you no doubt realize from reading this chapter, reducing your customers' costs requires in-depth knowledge and expertise. It seems like a lot of work, because it is. But keep in mind that the very fact that it is difficult is what will make the practice so rare—and valuable. You don't need to become an expert in all your customer's business processes, just those that, by virtue of the product or service you are selling, you can affect.

10

Effectiveness

Although you can make significant improvements to your customers' profits by lowering their costs, you will leave a lot of money on the table if you stop there. Always remember that cutting costs—though vital for business survival—is never the reason any company is in business. They are in business to produce value for their customers, and you will succeed in sales if you can help them increase that value and get paid for it. While every business process carries a cost, it also produces an effect. Our concern in this chapter is to help your customers improve or increase the effect of their business processes through the use of your product. If you are successful, the effects will show up as a raising of the slope on the top line of your profit wedge diagram.

To define "effectiveness," let's revisit the productivity equation we first looked at in Chapter 2, "Creating Value":

$$\text{Productivity} = \frac{\text{Output}}{\text{Input}} \times \text{Speed}$$

This simple mathematical relationship demonstrates that by concentrating on the top line of that equation, we can also add value to our customers and improve their productivity and profits.

In the last chapter, we looked for ways to help our customers remove resources from the cash flow engine, with a focus on reducing costs and eliminating "leakage" at various stages of the engine's performance. Efficiency is about subtraction. *Effectiveness,* on the other hand, is about addition, and even multiplication. The thought process is concerned with increasing output rather than decreasing inputs. Effectiveness is externally oriented; the business-improvement orientation shifts from internal processes to your customer's relationships with *their* customers. While efficiency talks about limiting costs, effectiveness talks about expanding the limits of an organization.[1]

Looked at in terms of the cash flow engine, effectiveness comprises two of the ways that we can increase cash flow: increase the size of the engine (revenues), and increase the difference between what it costs to create products and what the market will pay for those products (gross margins).

HELPING YOUR CUSTOMERS ADD VALUE

Hopefully by now you are thinking of your own business as being dedicated to improving your customers' cash flow engines. Extending that thought process, your customers are dedicated to the same goal in their businesses. To the extent that you can help them improve *their* customers' cash flow engines, you are adding value. The more your customers can add value to their own customers, the more effective they will be as organizations.

Your task, then, is to find as many ways as possible to use your product to help your customers add value to their customers. If you can do this, the payoff to your customers will come in the form of increased revenues and fatter gross profit margins. Effectiveness improvements include all those factors that relate to the amount of value your customer creates. The results will show up in two different ways in your customer's cash flow engine:

- Total revenues—Make the engine bigger by increasing the throughput. As you will see, this will require some combination of increasing demand for the company's products and increasing production to meet demand.
- Gross profits—Increase the size of the "buckets" that dip into the market. In other words, increase the difference between the

---

1. Peter Drucker, *Management: Tasks, Responsibilities, Practices*, Harper & Row, 1973.

cost of the product presented to the market, and the price the market is willing to pay for it.

WHY YOU NEED TO KNOW THIS

Often the primary emphasis of the buyers to whom you talk is cost reduction, and you can justify their investment in your product by concentrating on this area alone. However, that's not always the case, and even when it is, there are still good reasons for you to expand your own limits and go beyond cost cutting:

* Decision makers are increasingly shifting their focus from cost cutting to growth. The era of downsizing and reengineering is reaching its limits as companies find that they cannot downsize forever. Many have found that their cuts have gone too deep, slicing through fat and into muscle. Their ability to grow has been seriously curtailed, and corporations are discovering that they must reemphasize revenue growth. As a recent article in the *Wall Street Journal* expressed it: "It's the top line, stupid."[2] You will find a much more receptive audience than you have in the past. A survey taken in 1994 of CEOs of top companies reported in *Grow to Be Great* indicated that 94 percent of top executives polled considered growth a top priority.[3] As an American Management Association survey revealed in 1996, customer service and increasing revenues were the two top-ranked priorities of top executives, and reengineering had slipped to 16th place.[4] Remember, to be successful, you must think what they are thinking and talk about what they want to hear.
* Focusing on effectiveness can set you apart. Effectiveness improvements are usually more difficult to find and quantify than cost cutting, so your competitors are less likely to be discussing these issues with your prospects.

2. Greg Ip, "Sales Growth Becomes Challenge," *Wall Street Journal*, February 3, 1997, p. C1.
3. Dwight L. Gertz and Joao Baptista, *Grow to Be Great*, Free Press, 1995, p. 3.
4. Reported in Ronald Henkoff, "Growing Your Company: Five Ways to Do It Right!," *Fortune*, November 25, 1996, p. 78.

- You may be able to find more potential allies in the organization. Sometimes the people within your customer's organization who stand to gain from effectiveness improvements are different from those interested in greater efficiencies. If your product costs more than a competing solution, or will increase your customer's costs, you had better be prepared to show how the increased expenditure will be returned. To do that, however, you must be able to reach the right people within the organization: those who will benefit from the improvements.
- You will increase the perceived value of your solution. Sometimes your solution can cut costs and deliver higher revenues at the same time. Ignoring the effectiveness dimension might mean that you are leaving "money on the table."

WHY EFFECTIVENESS IMPROVEMENTS ARE SO HARD TO FIND

It is generally more difficult to find ways to improve a customer's effectiveness than their efficiency. One reason is habit. Prompted by the cost-cutting emphasis of their customers, many salespeople are simply conditioned to concentrate on cost savings. However, there is another, more subtle reason. As a thinking process, it is much easier to regard a situation, see what is there, and figure out what needs to be taken out, than to figure out what needs to be put in. Efficiency is about finding incremental improvements to existing processes; effectiveness questions whether the processes even need to be done at all. Efficiency improvements require analytical thinking, but effectiveness often requires imaginative thinking. This kind of thinking is made more important as technological capabilities make possible entirely new ways of doing business.

Because effectiveness is about helping your customers add value to their customers, you must know enough about how they do that in order to speak intelligently and imaginatively about using your product to help them. But this difficulty is what makes effectiveness improvements so powerful: you have a much better chance of being the first to point it out. The framework in this chapter will help you spot effectiveness-improvement opportunities.

THE COMPONENTS OF EFFECTIVENESS

Fortunately the components of effectiveness are relatively few: your customers are looking to sell more, which could be a problem of production or of marketing (or a combination of both), and to command a higher price for their products, relative to the cost of production.

Revenue

As your customers begin to focus on growing their top lines, they will be more receptive to revenue-improvement suggestions. To find opportunities for improvement, consider the dynamics of your customers' revenue, which are quite simple. Revenue improvements are the product of the volume of units sold times the price per unit:

$$\text{Revenue} = \text{Volume} \times \text{Price}$$

You may be able to show the effect of your product on either or both of the components on the right side of the equation, and the depth of your understanding of each will determine your success in increasing the value of your product in your customer's mind. Let's take a look at each in further detail.

Volume

Before you rush off to find ways to use your product to increase your customer's sales volume, you must first be sure whether the business has a production problem or a marketing problem. This is critical because the two problems are very different and require different solutions.

Every business strives to create a perfect match between demand and supply. In an ideal world, a firm would be able to sell all that it could produce, and produce all that it could sell. In real life, of course, it almost never works out that way. Some firms have excess production capacity—their principal challenge is to create enough demand to use their capacity. For these companies, your task is to help them with their marketing efforts. Other firms have a challenge in producing enough product to meet demand. Your challenge in this case is to help them increase production. While this may seem to be fairly simple to figure out for your customer, it can be more complicated than that. Firms with multiple product lines may wrestle with both aspects of the problem simultaneously. Even companies with only one product may wrestle with both problems, depending on demand, geography, the time of year, or even the time of day. This is especially true when the "inventory" disappears if it is not used—as in hotel rooms, airplane seats, technicians' expertise, or telephone airtime. Airlines are in a constant struggle between half-empty airplanes and overbooked flights. Sometimes they have to turn away full-fare business passengers because they have already sold those seats at a discount to leisure travelers, or seats go unsold because the carrier did not make available enough low-priced fares. It is a constant struggle for them to figure out exactly how much of each product will be demanded by customers at specific times.

These examples underscore the point that increasing revenues for your customers can involve two very different categories of problems. Sometimes they are looking for ways to sell more, and other times you need to help them produce more. The capabilities of your product will dictate which type of companies you will target, how you will approach your prospects, and who in the organization you will sell to.

Production

How can you squeeze more product or service out of a given unit of input? If you are talking to a manufacturing concern, your issue is to increase the throughput of widgets through the production pipeline. For a service corporation, it might involve finding a way for a technician to see one more customer per day. You must know your customers' production processes intimately and have a clear understanding of the impact of your solution, except now you focus on the outputs of the process rather than the inputs. Since Adam Smith wrote about the specialization of labor at a hypothetical pin factory, there have been entire libraries written about the challenges of increasing production, so this section is not about adding to that body of knowledge. However, some of the more important ways you can help your customers increase production are listed here to spark your imagination. Which apply to your solution?

- Improve inventory management
- Improve forecasting
- Take time out of the production process
- Take steps out of the production process
- Reduce time devoted to paperwork
- Shorten delivery time
- Shorten order-processing time
- Automate customization
- Approve customer credit faster
- Increase billable hours
- Improve scheduling
- Produce bigger units
- Make learning curves steeper
- Improve process yield
- Reduce rework

As you can infer from this partial list, there are literally thousands of ways to help your customers increase production. The more you know about your customers' production processes, the more ways you can find. The key is to focus on the general applications of your product and your customers' principal leverage points for production increases.

Marketing

The marketing challenge is the corollary of the production problem: how to help your customers increase the demand for their products so they can sell all they can produce. There are four general routes to increasing demand:

- *Improve the objective value of the product*—What can you do to make your customers' products more valuable to their customers or give the products a capability their competitors cannot match? If the product is something physical, you may be able to help the customer improve its functionality, perhaps by adding features, or improving existing performance, or you may help the company increase reliability. For customers selling a service, you might be able to help them deliver the service faster, more reliably, or more cheaply. (Efficiency improvements can also be shown to have the additional benefit of increasing effectiveness and revenues.) Another way to improve your customers' product is to help them innovate faster and more effectively. Anything that you can do that helps your customers get successful new designs into production faster, or customize their products for their customers, should result in higher revenues. Maybe you can help a company sell more of its more expensive products by adding functionality that appeals to higher market segments.

• *Improve the subjective value of the product (more effective sales and marketing)*—Another way to help your customers sell more is to help them with their sales and marketing efforts. What can you do to make your customer more effective in presenting the value of its products to the market? Does your solution help the company's sales force, for example? Perhaps you can improve the presentations or the image of the company's salespeople, or help them be more productive by seeing more prospects in the same amount of time, or extend the geographical reach of the sales force. Maybe your improvements to the product help your customers open up a market that was previously closed to them. Can you help their marketing efforts by improving the speed and reliability of information about their customers' needs or tastes, their competitors' moves? Maybe you can help them identify profitable and unprofitable customers, so that they can target ways to sell more to the former and get rid of the latter.

• *Improve the total solution value*—In looking for ways to make your customer's product more valuable to the market, do not confine your search to the tangible product itself. Think of as many ways as you can to help your customers improve the value they bring to their customers. You may find it useful to go back to the Total Solution Table in Chapter 8. You were introduced to it as a tool to help you broaden the definition of value that you bring to your customers, but you can also think about your customer's Total Solution Table. What can you do to help your customers increase the value they bring to their own customers at each phase of their own product life cycle? For example, at the implementation phase you may be able to make the product more convenient for customers to purchase or easier to install, or speed up the delivery. The heavy investments that companies have made in recent years in EDI and websites represent their efforts to enhance the value they offer their customers at the implementation phase by making it as easy as possible for their customers to figure out what they want and to buy it. As you will see in the next chapter, in some industries the ability to deliver earlier than the competition has allowed some companies to gain significant market share. At the support and growth phase, your solution might make the product more rugged and reliable, or give the business the ability to better serve customers or to fix problems faster. This is especially valuable in retaining profitable customers and in generating word-of-mouth referrals that are so valuable in creating demand. Any improvements you can make to your customer's ability to deliver value to its customers will help it sell more product. Go back to Chapter 8 and review the Total Solution Table, but this time from the point of view of your customer.

• *Remove impediments from the marketing, sales, and delivery of the product*—Often your customers know exactly what they could do to increase demand for their products, but they just do not have the technology or the resources to do it. Perhaps they do not have the ability to efficiently reach customers in a far-off geographic area, or they want to make the product easier to use, for example. It may be as basic as a bigger truck to make more deliveries without having to return to the warehouse, or as wide ranging as a flexible manufacturing system that allows the company to quickly customize its product for different customers.

Selling Price and Gross Profit

The second major factor affecting revenue is the average selling price of the company's product. If your customers can find ways to increase the average price of the products they sell, they may increase revenues, gross profits, or both, so this discussion leads us into the second major route to effectiveness improvements.

Gross Profit

If your customers will be happy with increased revenues, they will probably be ecstatic if you can show them how to increase the gap between what it costs to produce the goods or service and what they can get for it in the marketplace. We have already looked at ways of reducing the cost to produce; in this section we focus on the second half of that equation: increasing the selling price.

The accounting definition of gross profit is simply revenue minus the cost of goods sold. The conceptual definition, however, is that gross profit is the measure of how much value the company adds to the resources it takes in. For example, the market allows a certain gross profit margin to grocery stores for the service they provide in bringing together a vast variety of goods for consumption. Some of those same goods, however, command a much greater price in convenience stores because the market places greater value on convenience and speed. Similarly, a fancy restaurant adds value in terms of cachet or atmosphere and can command higher prices for comparable food in other restaurants (at least for the specific niche of the market that is attracted there).

As we have already seen, there are many routes the firm can take to increase the appeal of its products in the market. The business can then leverage those improvements into more sales—or higher prices. Often a higher gross profit margin is the preferred choice, because any increase to the sales price goes directly to the bottom line. Revenue increases derived from increased unit sales must be paid for by producing those extra units, but price increases come without that burden. Your customer's top management will make the strategic choice of revenue versus gross profit margin; your job is to know how to present the benefit depending on that choice.

Selling price is a very slippery subject, usually depending far more on subjective, psychological factors than on objective issues. That does not mean, however, that you cannot help your customer. There are many factors that you might be able to affect, including:

- More features
- Improved packaging
- Enhanced image
- Improved quality/reliability
- Improved premium product mix
- Easier/faster product customization
- Increased options
- Greater information content
- Greater customer convenience
- Switching costs
- Faster product customization

- Faster delivery
- More accurate marketing
- More effective sales presentations
- Higher trade-in value

Go over this list with a pencil in hand, and mark any of these areas that you can impact with your product.

Customer Satisfaction and Loyalty

So far, we have talked about ways to help our customers win new customers, but just as important to them is the necessity of hanging on to and generating more revenue from those they already have. Improvements in customer satisfaction are not as easy to measure as increases in sales volume or gross profits but are nevertheless an important component of effectiveness improvements. If effectiveness is a measure of how much value is added to customers, then increases in customer satisfaction would certainly indicate that customers perceive a lot of value. In the long run, of course, increases in customer satisfaction will show up in the standard effectiveness measurements. Satisfied customers are more frequent repeat buyers and generally spend more on average; they also tend to tell their friends about how happy they are, so revenue is increased. Additionally, they are generally less apt to comparison-shop, so the company can usually command higher gross profit margins when its customers are pleased with what they buy.

How can your product help your customers increase the satisfaction and loyalty of their customers? Add to the preceding list the following possibilities:

- Improve their communication with their customers, especially after the sale
- Help them shorten the delivery or implementation time from initial customer contact to satisfaction of their need (much more on this in the next chapter)
- Improve the range of options they can offer their customers
- Make it more convenient for their customers to purchase additional products
- Enable access to more information about their customers' needs

SELLING EFFECTIVENESS

Presenting your product or service in terms of effectiveness brings different challenges from promoting its efficiency. Generally you will be talking to different people within the organization, and you will be using "softer" numbers.

Oscar Wilde defined a cynic as "a man who knows the price of everything, and the value of nothing." Sometimes it seems that the purchasing managers you deal with fit that description exactly. In this context, it means that effectiveness improvements will be harder to sell to them than to others within the organization. Because they are measured by how much they cut costs, their focus will be almost exclusively on efficiency improvements. To be successful selling effectiveness, you will have to establish ties to others in the organization. The people who are most interested in effectiveness are the line managers who are responsible for marketing and sales, for gross profits, and for customer satisfaction. They are the "problem owners" who focus on the top line at least as much as the bottom line. The nature of their challenge is such that they are usually more open to visionary ideas about business improvement even when the ideas are unproven. That's the point of effectiveness improvements: they are usually about new ways of doing things, so it is more difficult to know in advance how much value they will bring.

It can be very difficult to quantify the value of effectiveness improvements because effectiveness is all about adding value to customers, and value is by definition very subjective. Effectiveness increases are always contingent on the behavior of your customers' customers, and behavior is always difficult to predict. While you can analyze a process and confidently forecast cost savings, effectiveness sometimes has to be taken at least partially on faith.

That is why it can be difficult to sell your product based on effectiveness improvements. Psychologically, people place a greater value on more concrete measurements, so in one sense your effectiveness improvements appear to bring less value than efficiency improvements. However, the fact that their value is less easy to predict does not mean that they are any less valuable. In fact, enhanced effectiveness is much more important to the organization's long-term corporate survival. To ensure that your customers buy in to the value of effectiveness, you must be positioned with people who are high enough in the organization to see the big picture and take a longer-term view of business improvements. Besides calling higher, make sure you target the operating levels and positions in the company: the people responsible for sales and market share, and those who interact with customers.

Because effectiveness improvements can be so difficult to predict, it is crucial to gain agreement on believable numbers. Find as many people as possible in the organization who are interested in increasing effectiveness, and get them to tell you what they expect the benefit of the system to be. Quantifying expected effectiveness improvements is much more of a "selling" job than demonstrating cost savings. There is a definite art to this process, which we will discuss in Chapters 13 and 14.

ACTION POINTS

Sometimes the difference between efficiency and effectiveness is perspective. A new machine that saves time in production can be sold as either a time saver or a revenue producer. How you present it depends on who is listening. As the old saying goes, "Where you stand on an issue depends on where you sit." There is a strong tactical advantage in seeing, and being able to present, both sides of the same coin. The more perspectives you bring to the problem and solution, the more potential allies you can find in your prospect's decision-making process.

To better see both sides, do the following:

1. Take a closer look at the advantages of your product and re-cast them in terms of effectiveness improvements for your customers in general.
2. For a specific customer, examine their decision process or organizational chart to determine the person or persons most likely to be interested in effectiveness improvements.
3. Gain agreement from that person on the value of the effectiveness improvements your solution can provide.

11

Speed

During the Civil War, Confederate cavalry general Nathan Bedford Forrest said the trick to war was to "Get there first with the most men." That approach would have helped him win a lot of business in today's economy, because in the past several years, a third front has opened up in the war for competitive advantage: *speed*. You have read here and in countless other books and articles about the rapid pace of change in our economy today. The key word there is *rapid*, especially in any segment of the economy that incorporates high technology. Companies are finding that they must move quickly just to keep up with their competitors and their customers' demands—not only to introduce innovative products faster but also to produce products, deliver goods, serve customers, or process claims much faster than they previously dreamed possible.

We have seen in previous chapters that every business process uses resources, and while some of those resources add value to customers, many do not. Time is one of the resources that is most wasted in business processes, and time truly is money, because speed has become the third imperative of business success. The old model used to be: produce a quality product at a reasonable price, and you are virtually assured of success in the marketplace. Those two requirements have not changed; it's just that now you have to deliver both exactly when the customer wants them.

Of course, one way to do that is to build up large inventories and store them near customers, creating buffers that let you respond quickly to their needs; the customers will not know any difference. The problem with that approach is that inventory is very expensive, and increasing the amount in the system actually slows down the cash flow engine. That means that, in order to respond faster, you are actually making the machine slower. There is a better way: *lower* inventory levels and work backlogs, and remove time from the entire system. Competing on the basis of time actually means competing *against* time.[1]

Referring back to our customer's cash flow engine, you will recall that the engine generates a certain amount of cash every time it turns over. You have already seen how effectiveness and efficiency improvements can increase the amount of cash generated with each turn of the engine. If you can also increase the speed of the engine, you can make a significant impact on the total cash thrown off.

The goal in improving your customer's speed of doing business is to get the company's engine to turn faster. If it generates the same amount of cash per turn but turns over more often in a year, more cash will be thrown off, which will either improve the bottom line of the income statement in the form of higher profits, or strengthen the balance sheet in the form of greater liquidity.

WHY YOU NEED TO KNOW THIS

Focusing on speed improvements for your customers adds a third dimension to the value proposition you bring to your clients, and will help your sales process in several ways.

Although improvements in the speed of your customer's business may seem to be a subset of efficiency improvements, time-based competition has become an important issue to many companies. Your customers are focusing more tightly on speed as a measure of business success than they have in the past. Buzzwords such as time-based competition and cycle-time reduction have become common elements in your customers' competitive lexicon. And, in the relentless logic of competition, the more tightly they focus on it, the more their competitors do also, forcing even greater efforts in that area. For example, now that just-in-time inventory management is commonplace, many firms are concentrating on "just-in-sequence," which requires inventory deliveries within hours of the need rather than a

1. Credit for this phrase goes to George Stalk Jr. and Thomas M. Hout, *Competing Against Time*, Free Press, 1990.

few days. In some firms, the emphasis on speeding up business processes is more than just another element in their quest for improvement: it is a declared cornerstone of their competitive strategy and their internal efforts for self-improvement. Here is an example from General Electric's 1993 annual report:

> Focusing on the order-to-remittance cycle—from time of order to when we get paid—has increased our inventory turns 27% in two years, throwing off almost $2 billion in cash in the process. Every single-digit improvement in inventory turns produces $1 billion in cash to reinvest for tomorrow.

That quote is representative of how seriously companies are viewing the prospect of reducing cycle times in their business. Cycle-time management, in effect, brings its own terminology to the language of value that your customers are looking for.

Couching your value in the language of speed improvements, therefore, adds another set of tools to your tool kit for adding value to your customer. This can help you to increase the value of your solution in your customer's eyes, and it may also help you expand the range of potential contacts in the customer's organization who have a business problem you can solve.

As you will see below, finding ways to improve the speed of your customer's business processes can translate directly into profit improvements, increases in the company's cash position, and improvements to the company's competitive position.

Finally, although cycle-time management is no longer a revolutionary topic in business, it is still new enough that the average salesperson, even if focusing on financial improvements, is probably not focusing on it. Paying attention to speed will help set you apart from your competitors.

THE VALUE OF SPEED

The firm that can speed up its business processes and deliver value to its customers faster can benefit in several ways:

• *Higher revenues and profits*—Every time the cash flow engine completes one revolution, it generates a profit. (At least, that's the object.) All things being equal, increasing the number of revolutions made during the year will produce higher revenues, and profits will increase at least in proportion to the acceleration. The greatest benefit of cycle-time improvements, though, is that *all things do not remain equal.* Increasing response time brings a number of benefits to companies and their customers which adds to their appeal in the marketplace. Studies have shown that companies can achieve response times that are three or four times faster than their competitors', and the net result of doing so is that they "grow three times faster than the average for the industry and will be twice as profitable as the average for all competitors."[2] Some of the fastest-growing companies of recent years, including Dell in computers and Wal-Mart in retail, have made their mark by time-based competition.

• *Increased cash flow*—As you saw in Chapter 5, the amount of assets held by your customers can be expressed in terms of days. Given the firm's total revenues, and knowing how much inventory it has on hand, for example, will allow you to calculate how many days worth of inventory it carries. The relationship also works in the other direction: if the company can move inventory faster through the cycle, it will need less total inventory to generate the same amount of revenue. This can free up a tremendous amount of cash, as you saw in Chapter 9. It takes time to deliver value to customers, from initial discovery of the customer's need to receipt of payment for satisfying that need. Every day that can be removed from that time can be directly converted into cash benefits for your customers.

You've heard the old expression that time is money. In this case there is a simple way to put a price on it. To calculate how much a day's cash flow is worth to your customer, simply divide the company's total revenues by 365.

For example, if your customer is a $1 billion company, each day it generates just under $3 million in sales. If you can show the customer how to remove just one day from an order-to-remittance cycle of 90 days, it is potentially worth $3 million in additional cash flow, which can probably go a long way toward justifying the investment in your solution!

• *Higher gross profits*—Many companies have proved that they can command higher prices for their products simply by delivering them

2. Stalk and Hout, p. 4.

faster or guaranteeing the actual time of delivery. One reason is economic: their customers value the speed and reliability of delivery enough to compensate for higher prices. Because speed becomes one of the benefits they offer to their customers, they are able to differentiate their products enough to avoid strict price competition. If your customer's sales force is adept at pointing out to their customers the financial benefits of faster deliveries, such as lower safety stocks, smoother production runs, or less wasted time, they will be able to justify higher profit margins for their products. If they are not, give them a copy of this book.

The new-product cycle is one of the most important processes for achieving benefits from cycle-time reduction. If your customer can get a new product to market faster than anybody else, it will in effect have a monopoly until its competitors can respond. This will allow it to enjoy premium pricing for at least a short time.

There are also subjective reasons that speed can improve gross profit margins. The company's reputation for speed and responsiveness is a tremendous boost to its image in the marketplace. In addition, newer products are generally better and more sophisticated—sometimes fresher—and thus able to command higher price premiums.

• *Increased market share*—Because customers are demanding faster speeds from the companies they do business with, they will turn away from those that can't keep up with their demands. The disadvantage of American car companies relative to the Japanese in the rate of new model introductions, and in manufacturing and delivery, was one of the major contributors to their steady loss of American market share. By the same token, those that make the grade will find that market share is theirs for the taking. FedEx was probably one of the first to prove this, but many other companies in different industries are following its lead.

So many corporate customers are following just-in-time inventory practices nowadays that those suppliers who can meet their demands will win the bulk of their business. In order to compete profitably, however, they will need to respond to their customers' demands for speed with improvements in their own throughput. Simply piling up inventories to meet their customers' JIT inventory needs is an extremely expensive way to conduct their business. Additionally, some companies are looking for ways to optimize the entire supply chain, reasoning that unless inefficiencies are squeezed out of all levels, those costs will eventually be passed on to consumers anyway. As a result, your customers may find that competing on speed is more than a way to improve their business: it is a necessity for survival.

Speed also includes innovation and time to market with new products. The company getting to market first can reap significant first-mover advantages. In some industries, such as computer hardware and software, being first to market could make that company's product the de facto standard; in effect, there is no second place.

• *Greater customer satisfaction*—Some companies have done such a good job in speeding up their processes that they are achieving astounding turnaround times in fulfilling orders and servicing products, and their performance is winning them customers for life. For example, the notebook computer on which this manuscript is being typed had a problem with its screen about a month ago. When I called the manufacturer's help line, they sent an overnight package service to pick it up on a Friday afternoon, repaired the screen, and delivered it back to my door on Tuesday morning. They have certainly cemented my loyalty, and—as an added bonus—two of the many people I told that story to have already purchased computers from the company as a result.

Retailers that compete on speed find that they can stock a wider variety of fresher products, and respond faster to changing consumer demand, which keeps customers happily returning to their stores.

• *Greater efficiencies*—Focusing on speeding up operations may seem expensive, but the emphasis on speed can make a company more efficient and lower its overall costs if it is done correctly. Many firms have found that working with very lean inventories has exposed numerous inefficiencies that had previously been hidden by generous cushions of raw materials and spare parts. The painful process of learning how to operate under such demanding conditions helps to whip their operations into shape.

• *Lower risk*—The ability to respond quickly to changing market conditions or unexpected opportunities helps companies lower the risk they face in pursuing a particular course of action. Companies that can make adjustments quickly are less at risk from mistakes, because they can fix the problem or shift direction before the damage gets too great.

Speed of operations also translates into lower lead times for inventory production, which can make forecasting more accurate. This can be a significant advantage in markets where inventory is subject to fashion, technical obsolescence, or spoilage. A smaller cushion also helps in spotting changes in market acceptance or customer needs.

As you can see, many of the benefits added by cycle-time reduction can also be expressed in the language of effectiveness and efficiency, but time-based competition has become such an important business strategy that it makes sense to treat it as a third dimension of value. In fact, firms are finding that applying a cycle-time focus to their business processes may expose some expensive fallacies in the old style of thinking. For example, a focus on efficiency dictates that machines be used to their maximum capacity. It makes sense from that point of view: spreading the costs of the machine over more units lowers the cost per unit. The problem with that idea is that it can lead to costly buildups of unnecessary inventory or bottlenecks somewhere down the line. In other words, while the quest for efficiency might dictate strengthening individual links in the chain, cycle-time reduction dictates a focus on *throughput*, which provides a broader perspective in which consequences across the entire value chain are considered. It can lead to the seemingly paradoxical yet valid conclusion that it makes sense to run certain processes more slowly than they are capable of running, in order to speed up the entire process. A focus on speed will cause decision makers to look at the entire chain.

The rest of this chapter explains the individual cycles that make up your customer's cash flow engine, with examples of how various firms have realized benefits from accelerating each cycle; the chapter concludes with suggestions of ways that you may be able to apply your product to cut time from each cycle. But first, it is important to introduce some of the vocabulary of speed that your customers use so you can recognize the need when these terms come up during your sales cycle.

THE LANGUAGE OF SPEED

The quest for cycle-time reduction in companies has engendered its own vocabulary and collection of acronyms, so if you are to speak the language of speed, you should be prepared to use the following terms intelligently. Moreover, when you hear these from your customers or see them in their annual reports, it will be a tip-off that they are looking for benefits in this dimension.

Build to Order—A more extreme variation of a *pull system*, in which the unit is not even produced or assembled until the customer has ordered it. Dell proved this was possible in the personal computer market, and its success has compelled the competition to play on Dell's terms and try to match it.

Continuous Replenishment Process (CRP)—One of several systems designed to streamline the supply chain. Point-of-sale information triggers production at manufacturing plants even before an order is generated by the customer.

Efficient Consumer Response (ECR)—A strategy of supply-chain optimization that attempts to slash time from the entire supply chain, by integrating strategies and processes of all the companies involved. Information about consumer demand is communicated instantly to all levels of suppliers so that they may act more in concert.

Electronic Data Interchange (EDI)—A system that links suppliers and purchasers electronically so that orders can be generated quickly, without paperwork. In some advanced examples, suppliers and customers might actually have access to some components of the other's computer systems, in order to further strengthen the communication and coordination of needs.

Flexible Manufacturing Systems—The traditional manufacturing practices emphasize long production runs and minimum changeovers, and any production not immediately demanded by customers is stored in warehouses, whereas flexible manufacturing systems are driven by actual demand and require quick changeovers and short production runs. The net benefit is faster response to customer needs and lower inventories.

Just-In-Sequence—A more extreme and demanding version of *just-in-time* that may require inventory deliveries several times a day.

Just-In-Time (JIT)—A strategy of production that requires suppliers to deliver raw materials in small amounts, directly to where they are needed, when they are needed.

Pull System—Traditional systems driven by efficiency and economies of scale are "push" systems, with inventories being produced in large-lot sizes and pushed out to the consumer.

Because the consumer is not always ready to comply with the schedule dictated by efficiency, excess inventories tend to pile up along the way, in warehouses and on store shelves. A pull system, on the other hand, is based on actual consumption. The purchase of a unit is the trigger that alerts producers upstream to produce a replacement. (You may also hear the term *kanban* system, which is the Japanese word for it.)

PROCESSES TO SPEED UP

Just as an automobile engine has many moving parts, your customer's cash flow engine is one complete cycle that is made up of many smaller cycles and processes. Although just about every business process that your customer executes probably has room for cycle-time improvements, there are several horizontal processes in which cycle-time improvements are more likely to be found and where the ability to do so can make an important impact on the customer's cash flow engine:

- Product design (time to market)—Designing a new product is much more involved than just having engineers sit in an office and design the latest and greatest mousetrap. They must communicate often with upper management, marketing, sales, production, and all the other departments that may have an interest in the design of the product and will affect its acceptance in the marketplace. Often the product-introduction process entails several iterations, in which someone down the line reviews the latest effort and returns it with questions and suggested modifications. Every iteration takes time just to communicate and then requires time going back to the drawing board for another try. For especially complicated products, teams of designers may have to get involved for even the most minute changes.
- Supply chain management—The cash flow engine shows cash flowing into inventory, but it does not really depict exactly how much time can elapse during that process. The raw materials that are in position to be processed or assembled have been in movement or in storage for many days just to get where they are; and the flow of information that took place to get them there

was probably even more extensive, including meeting with suppliers' sales representatives, selecting the best suppliers, placing orders, waiting for them to deliver, and literally dozens of other steps. After the materials have undergone the production process, that movement continues downstream. A complete supply chain may run from suppliers to the manufacturer, then on to distribution, from there to retail stores, and finally to the consumer. Your customer could fit into any one or several of these categories. A retail store, for example, will demand just-in-time inventory deliveries from distributors. If the distributors achieve that level of service by piling up inventories, it is a costly way to do it, and those costs will eventually be passed on to the consumer. So, the search for every penny of cost advantage is leading many companies to figure out ways to optimize the entire supply chain. They realize that making their upstream suppliers and their downstream customers more efficient can help everybody in the entire chain. If your suppliers are more efficient, they will be able to furnish your suppliers at a lower cost, and you in turn will be able to pass on lower costs to your customers, leading to more sales, and a win-win situation for all involved. More important than local improvements, however, is the ability to improve information and product flows across the entire chain, to make the whole process work more smoothly, with less disruption.

- Production—Although production processes have been studied and improved since the beginning of the Industrial Revolution, firms are always finding new ways to improve them, especially as information technology provides newer and better tools. The fact is, the typical production process even in the best plants still offers numerous opportunities for cycle-time reduction. In *Lean Thinking*, for example, the authors show how the typical production process can consist of 90 percent or more wasted time.[3] Similarly, one study in *Competing Against Time* indicated that, "in traditional manufacturing systems, products usually receive value for only .05% to 5% of the time they are in the system."[4] Only a minute portion of the cycle time is actually spent adding

3. James P. Womack and Daniel T. Jones, *Lean Thinking*, Simon and Schuster, 1996.
4. Stalk and Hout, p. 49.

value to the product. The rest of the time, raw materials or work in process will pile up somewhere until the material can be moved to a different machine or assembly area, or until somebody can get around to doing something to it. Production does not have to involve a physical product, either. Consider a mortgage application. It may take weeks to get a decision, and then more weeks before closing, but the actual time spent processing the application is probably less than a few hours.

- Sales cycle—As a sales professional, you are no doubt well acquainted with the huge opportunities for reducing the amount of time taken in the average sales cycle. In the typical months-long sales cycle, you may actually spend less than a week's worth of actual time on that sales opportunity. Much of your time is spent waiting for calls to be returned, for data to be analyzed so that decisions can be made, for information to be gathered to complete a proposal, and so on. Shortening the sales cycle does more than give the salesperson increased time to close additional sales: every day that you do not close the business gives the competitor another chance to win it.
- Order fulfillment—When a customer orders a product, it sets into motion a chain of events involving different departments and functions. Perhaps the customer's credit must be checked and approved, the factory may have to be notified to begin assembling the system, the contract may have to go to the legal department for approval, accounting must generate an invoice and enter the accounting information, and the product must be shipped.
- Accounts receivable collection—The longest component of time in this process is the most difficult to control: waiting for the customer to pay. However, there is room for improvement in the time it takes to generate and mail an invoice, and to process the payment when it comes in.
- Customer service and complaint resolution—This is a process in which reductions in cycle time can have a huge impact on customer satisfaction and market share. Chapter 14 has an extended example of this.
- Management decision making and learning—This is not a discrete process within the company; it cuts across all the processes we have discussed and also includes all the support and admin-

istrative activities. Information flows through the company about suppliers, customers, and internal processes and activities, and managers must coordinate, guide, and sometimes direct the actions of all concerned. This information not only is critical for making decisions but also contributes to the firm's learning and creation of intellectual capital. The company that can learn faster about its customers, markets, competitors, technologies, and internal processes will have a definite advantage. The quest for speed emphasizes rapid collection of information and dissemination to the right people as well as prompt decision making, as close to the customer as possible. Your customers will welcome any product or service that gets the relevant information to the correct people in the least time.

SPEEDING UP THE PROCESSES

To reduce the cycle time of your customers' business processes, there are several contributions you might be able to make:

- Speed up specific activities—Perhaps your system can help your customer shave the time it takes to complete specific steps by helping the process move faster or take fewer steps.
- Eliminate activities—Any steps you can remove from the process reduce the total time by the amount it takes to complete those activities, plus the handoff time. The most fruitful improvements, however, can come from doing something differently in an upstream activity that will eliminate the need for activities downstream.
- Simplify processes—Many business processes are much more complicated than they need to be. Often the processes have grown over time beyond the need for specific steps. As processes become simpler, there is the obvious benefit of fewer steps requiring less time. Other benefits may be even more significant: fewer errors, and steeper learning curves, with productivity improving much faster.
- Improve first-pass quality—Much of the time wasted in production processes is in detecting and fixing previous mistakes.

- Allow activities to be performed concurrently—Much of the time wasted in any business process is generated by the need for one group to wait until a portion of the process is completed and then "thrown over the wall" for the group's input. Improved communications among groups involved in the process can enable them to work together. Ford Motor has taken advantage of "groupware" and videoconferencing technologies to enable engineers in different parts of the world to collaborate on car designs, for example.
- Substitute different activities—Perhaps you can show your customer how your technology can help it do something differently, which might make the process faster.
- Reduce fragmentation—Your solution might help your customer group related activities more intelligently, either in space or in time.
- Improve communication among the performers of different activities—We have already seen how a decision that makes sense in isolation can have a strong negative impact on the time it takes to perform downstream activities. Improved communications among groups can significantly reduce cycle times by helping participants keep an eye on the big picture.
- Improve the measurement of time taken by specific activities— It is a truism of management that what gets measured gets done. Giving people a window into their own performance provides feedback which can prompt them to improve performance. There are other types of information that can be useful if the information is recycled faster. Every cycle generates feedback about its results, and the faster that feedback is translated into improvements to the next cycle, the better the cycle will be and the shorter the learning curves. This is as true for internal customers as for external customers.

ACTION POINTS

To employ the "Get there first" concept with your customer, begin by looking for clues that the company might be especially receptive to a sales approach based on speed. You may find explicit references in its annual report, or certain clues in the business strategies that the company is pursuing. Perhaps you will recognize a need in jargon used in its publications or marketing materials, or by company executives when you meet with them.

Perhaps your previous sales experience has given you excellent insight and knowledge about your customers' business processes, albeit from the standpoint of effectiveness and efficiency improvements. If so, you should be able to translate that knowledge fairly easily into the language of speed improvements. All you have to do is shift your focus slightly and measure your contribution in terms of time as well as dollars. This might help you find additional justification for your solution, or it could suggest additional questions to ask. Finally, it could even help you find other allies within the organization, people who are concerned with speeding up business processes and who would welcome the opportunity to consider another tool to help them.

If you do not know your customers' businesses well enough yet, the previous discussion can give you a useful framework for spotting potential opportunities for business improvement. Keeping in mind the last few pages, ask yourself the following questions:

- Which of my customers' business processes can my solution affect?
- Which of the methods can I use to speed up those processes?
- What do I need to know about each process in order to credibly demonstrate the value of my solution?
- How many days can I remove from the process?
- What is that worth to the customer? (Cash flow, revenues, gross profits, or lower costs.)
- What proof do I have that it can be done?
- Who stands to benefit from improvements to that process?

Your solution does not have to apply across a customer's entire enterprise to make an important impact on the company's cash flow engine. As you saw at the beginning of this chapter, shaving one day from the cycle can give your customer back a lot of the cash tied up in inventory or other assets. That is why speed is a dimension of business value that you cannot afford to overlook.

12

The Strategic Fit

Although we have been concentrating throughout most of this book on the financial justification of your solution, benefits do not always have to be financially measurable to be important to your customer. There is another level of business value you can provide to your customers which is not as easy to quantify. You can provide many benefits to your customers for which you may not be able to quantify the value but that common sense tells the customer are excellent investments anyway. Remember, besides helping your customers solve business problems, your goal is to help them achieve their goals, and not all of them are easily quantifiable in dollar terms. Although all business goals theoretically support the company's profit and stockholder value imperatives, some of them may be expressed in different terms.

A customer may have one or more strategic goals that it fervently hopes to achieve, including fulfilling its vision statement and executing some broad business strategies. Typically these goals are expressed and pursued at the executive decision-making levels in the customer's organization and may provide the framework for targets, problems, and decisions at lower levels. For example, a CEO may decide to enter and dominate a specific market within a given time frame. This desire may be communicated to operating levels in the company that are responsible for creating plans and specific, dated targets for achieving certain milestones and financial results. In creating their plans, the operating units will assay their existing resources and capabilities, and make arrangements to fill the perceived gaps. These arrangements include specific projects that may

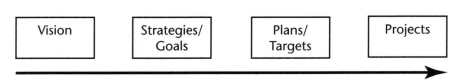

Figure 12-1.   Process for Pursuit of Strategic Goals

require the use of your product to make them successful. The thought process looks like Figure 12-1.

Up to now, we have been focusing primarily on specific results and financial targets, but if you want to be successful at the highest levels, it also helps to keep the strategic fit in mind. Often, when the strategy has already been decided, investment in the project is a given, and financial justification is not critical to the investment. In effect, it has already been justified, even if specific numbers are not used.

In information technology, for example, a trend in recent years has been to emphasize the strategic fit of information technology investments. Faced with the difficulty of predicting exactly how large investments in systems will impact the company financially, top executives are stressing the need to ensure that the investment's justification be expressed in terms of how it will contribute to corporate goals. That helps to account for the growing ranks of executives with primarily business, rather than engineering, backgrounds in the chief information officer slot. Companies are increasingly looking for Chief Information Officers (CIOs) with the ability to align technology strategy with business strategy. This state of affairs suggests that a well-informed sales professional can be an important ally to the CIO needing to validate important decisions to the board of directors.

Empirical support for this view is found in a recent survey that quizzed chief information officers and other senior managers on their cost-justification processes for high-tech investments. When asked where they saw the real opportunities for client/server networked computing, only 30 percent indicated business cost savings as the primary consideration, with the remaining 70 percent stressing the strategic value of the investment.[1] Strategic fit, then, is the "high road" to making the business case for your solution. It is not a substitute for financial justification, but it is a valuable complement.

1. Reported in Don Tapscott, *The Digital Economy*, McGraw-Hill, 1996, p. 119.

Business is a game that is relentlessly numbers oriented: the ultimate arbiter of success or failure is the result reflected in the bottom line and in the company's market value. However, many business executives, especially at top management levels, know that some decisions are right even if they cannot forecast the result of the decision with any accuracy. Some investments may enable them to take advantage of a new technology before their competition does, for example, or keep up with a competitor who has already adopted it. Faced with the chance to seize an opportunity to gain or maintain business advantage, they will take action first and worry about financial justification later. They govern themselves by the old saying "It is better to be roughly right than precisely wrong." For some business investments, the time spent gathering detailed information and making "precise" forecasts can cost more than it is worth, so—like horseshoes and atom bombs—"close" is good enough. The rush to the Internet by corporate America in the last two or three years is a case in point. Nobody was sure what the payoff—if any—would be, but nobody wanted to take a chance and perhaps get left out of the next "paradigm."

As business executives' principal concerns shift from cost cutting to revenue increases and other components of corporate effectiveness, moreover, it becomes more difficult to predict and measure the benefits of specific investments. In many cases common sense tells the decision makers that the investment will help the business. One survey of network managers at 41 firms showed that "most of them *assumed* (my italics) that benefits would follow from projects."[2] After all, if quantifiable business cases were required for every investment, the business world would not have training, public relations, prestigious offices, or even many unproved technologies.

New technologies make the task even more difficult. Until the technology is introduced and actually used in the real world, nobody can be certain exactly how it will perform, how people will react to it, or how people will actually use it. There is even a term for it in economics—the law of unforeseen consequences. So, how does anything new get sold? Fear: many firms do not want to take the chance and wait for others to try it and then see how it works for them.

2. Joseph E. Maglitta, "Beyond ROI," *Computerworld*, October 27, 1997, p. 73.

However, in those cases where strategic considerations govern the final decision, there nevertheless appears to be a need to create some form of financial justification even if there is not a strong faith in the reliability of the numbers. In the same CIO survey cited earlier, when asked to reflect on the business cases for investments that had been made in the past, 84 percent of respondents admitted that cost savings was the primary factor; only 16 percent mentioned the strategic dimensions.[3]

What does that mean for you as a salesperson? In order to maximize the attractiveness of your product as an investment alternative versus the competition, you must be prepared to do both: justify your investment in strategic terms, and back up your cost justification wherever possible with a "hard-dollar" quantification of your benefits.

FOCUS ON STRATEGIC QUESTIONS

Often you can justify the investment in your solution by its contribution to specific business goals and strategies rather than in hard-dollar terms, or in addition to the financial justification. That is why Chapter 3 introduced a series of questions, some of which concerned the customer's business goals, strategies, and initiatives, to keep in mind as you study your client's annual report. The answers to those questions will tell you about targets at which your customers are aiming that you might be able to help them hit.

Vision Statement

All self-respecting companies nowadays seem to have a vision or a mission statement, a concise description of what business they are in and what they expect to achieve in that business. You may think that some of these statements are simply a collection of platitudes and ambiguous buzzwords, which are justly skewered in Dilbert cartoons, and some clearly fit that description. In many cases, however, they are designed and actually serve as a call to action to rally the troops and provide a common purpose to thousands of employees

---

3. Tapscott, p. 119.

pursuing individual goals. Although you should not neglect the financial justification, you will strengthen your case, especially at higher management levels, if you can also demonstrate how your solution can move them closer to their vision. I personally have found it very effective to make a connection between the company's vision statement and my product in my introductory correspondence to top executives. Vision statements can also exist for individual business units or departments within the company.

Business Strategies

Business strategies are the path by which your customer navigates through its business environment to reach its vision, and are therefore more quantifiable and concrete. Although there is only one company vision, there may be several strategies to support it. Some strategies may talk about execution: improving cycle time, or quality initiatives, or JIT inventory; some may address markets: penetrating the corporate IT environment, or winning 10 points of market share, or increasing the percentage of revenue from services; some center around people: attracting and retaining the best people, pushing decision-making authority outward, and so on.

Because business strategies are more specific than the company mission statement, they often have specific metrics assigned, by which managers are able to measure progress along the strategy. If you can connect your solution to improvements in those measurements, that will go a long way toward justifying the investment, even if tangible dollar forecasts are not available. The added benefit of tying into business strategies is that there is often a "problem owner" to be found: the individual tasked with the responsibility to execute the strategy. That person could become your best ally in the organization.

RISK

As discussed in the Introduction, today's business environment is as volatile as ever, and no company can afford to get complacent about its position in its industry. In an economy that has enshrined paranoia as a management principle even at firms as successful as Intel, you can be sure that your customers will be concerned about business risk. Technology can overturn established industry leaders seemingly overnight, and running the cash flow engine at higher and higher speeds and closer tolerances exposes a company to problems. Just-in-sequence inventory management, for example, leaves a company vulnerable to traffic problems, weather, and strikes. When UPS workers went on strike in 1997, it had the greatest impact on firms that were the most efficient.

Although the cash flow engine is a powerful tool to model the benefits your customers are looking for, it suffers from one weakness: it does not account for risk. In the context of this chapter, we discuss business risk, which can have two meanings, both of which are important to decision makers. First, risk is the chance that bad things will happen. Second, it is deviation from expected results, either positive or negative. (There is a third meaning in the business context—investment risk: the odds that your solution will or will not deliver the promised results. Investment risk and strategies for dealing with it are discussed in Chapter 15.) In this chapter, we will focus on ways that you might be able to lower your customer's business risk.

The list of potentially harmful or even disastrous occurrences that worry your customers is extensive and includes the following classes of risk:

- Market risk
- Competitive risk
- Technological risk
- Legal risk
- Political risk
- Financial risk
- Credit risk
- Environmental risk
- Natural perils

Before we turn to specific ways to lower your customer's business risk, keep in mind that any enhancements to the customer's effectiveness, efficiency, and speed can also help to lower the customer's risk, even if only indirectly. Rising revenues and profits can cover a lot of sins by making the company stronger and better able to withstand shocks. Lowering costs does the same thing as well as limiting potential exposure. It also buys back time: by reducing the leakage from the bucket, the company in effect has more time to craft an effective response to crises. Lowering asset levels is also useful. For example, lean inventories reduce the risk of obsolescence or spoilage. Speeding up business processes can make the company more nimble and able to respond quickly to changing conditions. As you tally up the benefits you have found so far, be sure to include the effect on business risk.

To find leverage points for reducing risk, you can refer back to your answers about the customer's principal risks and challenges in Chapter 3. Or you can examine potential risks in finer detail, concentrating on the horizontal business process or the vertical division over which you have an impact.

It is very difficult or even impossible to measure the value of risk reduction. By its nature, risk deals with unforeseen or unforeseeable events. Ironically, often the only way to measure the value of risk reduction is to count the costs if it fails.

Your solution might be able to help your customer cope with risk in one of two ways: either reduce the chances of negative events occurring, or mitigate their effects if they do.

Here are a few of the principal opportunities for helping your customers reduce their business risk:

- Information—Faster access to better-quality information can go a long way toward reducing risk. The sooner decision makers know about changes, either positive or negative, the faster they can form a response. And, the more complete the information they have, the better the odds of an effective response. For example, improving communications with personnel in the field can help the company spot problems or opportunities faster. There is a lot of value in avoiding surprise. Remote or automatic monitoring devices that measure the health and performance of devices are another example.
- Insurance—You may be able to provide insurance against potential disasters through backup systems, disaster-recovery plans, other ways of doing the same thing, or alternative sources of supply.
- Safety—Anything that increases the safety of people and assets can also go a long way toward reducing risk. Protecting assets is measurable not only in terms of the replacement or repair cost of

the assets but also in terms of the potential lost business or productivity as a result of the company's not being able to use the
asset. When you talk about personal safety, the value is immea-
surable in one sense, of course, but it may be measured in the
forms of lower insurance rates, personal productivity, legal bills,
and litigation losses.
- Security—Security is closely related to safety but also includes
  crimes against property such as theft, and preservation of corporate secrets.
- Flexibility—You may also be able to increase customers' flexibility and agility. If they can respond quickly to changing conditions, the amount of exposure can be limited. If your product is
  easily customizable or adaptable, you may be able to connect
  that capability to increased flexibility for your customers.

In looking for ways to avoid or mitigate risk for your customer, you
may be more successful if you make sure to focus on your complete
product. Often many of your extended or potential product
attributes may be significant differentiators when expressed in terms
of their risk-lowering qualities. Obvious examples are financing
arrangements, guarantees, and after-sale support. Less obvious may
be such factors as your company's reputation and longevity. For years
it was commonly accepted that nobody ever got fired for buying IBM.
Don't sell yourself short, either. Your expertise and professionalism
may also be significant contributors.

COMPETITIVE NECESSITY

Remember that one of the biggest benefits you can provide to your
customer is competitive advantage: the tools to succeed in a volatile
and cutthroat environment. There is nothing like your customer's
competitor to convince the company that it should purchase your
solution. If you are introducing a new technology, for example, your
customer may decide to at least invest in a pilot project in order to
gain a competitive advantage. Even if your customers are not convinced that your product will make a significant difference, there is
always the chance that it might. Besides, if they do not do it, there is
the chance that their competitors will and be successful with it. For

example, many banks have invested large sums in on-line services to offer electronic banking to their customers. While these investments have yet to generate a profit, no one wants to take the chance that competitors will steal a march on the company and stake out a dominant position in cyberspace. Business rivals often act like the United States and the Soviet Union during the Cold War. No promising military technology was ignored by either side for fear that the other would gain even a minuscule advantage.

In very competitive industries, there is often a herd instinct. Each company is so afraid it will miss the next big advantage that it will throw money at new technologies or fads just because somebody else is doing it. The resulting rush can lead to the "tornado effect" as described by marketing consultant Geoff Moore. If you can get your product to that stage, you will be so busy trying to keep up with demand that selling will be the least of your worries. That's not a bad situation for a salesperson to be in, as long as they don't change your commission plan! The trick, however, is that to get to that stage, you have to convince a few early adopters to take the plunge. You can do that only if you can make a strong business case to justify the risk of investing in an unproven technology.

PEOPLE IMPACT

Many times a firm will make a large investment—such as training—purely for the expected positive impact on the morale, attitudes, and knowledge of its people, or for an even vaguer term: corporate culture. Although companies may find it very difficult to draw a tangible connection between their investment and some specific corporate measure such as increased sales or profitability, they make the investment anyway. Investments that improve the skills, knowledge, morale, comfort, or satisfaction of employees are seen as being of tremendous value by the corporation even when their impact cannot be measured directly.

That is not to say that it is impossible to make a quantifiable business case from the expected impact on a company's employees. Some companies have proved that they can do just that. Sears, for example, devised measurements—albeit after much time, effort, and experimentation—that directly connected improvements in employee attitudes to revenue growth. They showed that a 5-unit increase in employee attitude for a specific store, as measured by surveys, reliably translated into a 1.3-unit increase in "customer impression," which caused a 0.5 percent increase in revenue growth.[4]

Sometimes the company will have a specific strategy for improving or changing the attitudes or culture of the organization. Initiatives in this area include empowerment, knowledge management, creating teams, and fostering an entrepreneurial spirit.

Even investments that are made for their measurable impact on business performance may have positive side benefits on the users and others connected with the solution. Providing state-of-the-art equipment sends a strong message about the commitment of the corporation to do whatever is necessary to compete and to give its people the proper tools. Purchases such as cellular telephones and laptop computers can also be seen as perquisites of the job by sales or service people. As you add up the benefits you bring to your customers, don't hesitate to mention these as added "intangible" benefits.

QUALITY

Quality programs have become commonplace at American firms. If you have done a complete job in showing the impact of your solution on efficiency, effectiveness, and speed, you have probably already covered the benefits of quality for your customer. But, since quality programs sometimes take on a life of their own and engender their own disciples with their jargon and specific quality measurements, you may see some benefit from expressing your value in the language of quality.

IMAGE

If there is one thing that corporate executives really care about, it is the image of their company. Some are obsessed with how they are perceived by the general public, the business community, other executives, customers, or competitors. This quest for image can lead to

---

4. Anthony J. Rucci, Steven P. Kirn, and Richard T. Quinn, "The Employee-Customer-Profit Chain at Sears," *Harvard Business Review*, January–February 1998, p. 91.

many investment decisions that you can bet were never put through the "ROI" test before the money was spent. The more obvious include gleaming corporate headquarters buildings, "mahogany row" executive offices, corporate jets, and Super Bowl parties. However, even some more "practical" investments have their corporate-image benefits also. Being the first to install the latest and greatest software, or being the first airline to fly the new airliner, is frequently not the least of the reasons for these classes of investments.

The fact that an investment has the added benefit of enhancing the corporate image does not mean that it cannot be justified in financial terms. There may be tangible performance benefits (which are often the "official" justification) arising from other attributes of the product. The image associated with the product can have important practical benefits as well. As your customers strive to differentiate their products, their customers will judge them on two principal criteria: use criteria and signaling criteria.[5] Their customers (and yours) will evaluate potential investments based on how they will affect their corporate performance, to be sure; but they will also look for more subtle signals that will reassure them that the vendor with which they are dealing is successful, stable, and capable. Signaling criteria can be as varied as advertising; packaging; reputation; longevity; appearance of people, equipment, and premises; and so on. As a sales professional, when you buy that expensive new suit, you are investing in signaling criteria. At the corporate level, investments that bring signaling criteria benefits include sales force automation, telemarketing and customer service software, new vehicles, cosmetic enhancements to the end product, and the like.

ACTION POINTS

Unless you are comfortably positioned at the highest levels within your customer's organization, justifications based on strategic fit are best seen as complements to a hard business case. Do not neglect this dimension, but do not rely on it exclusively. Just as you have done in the previous three chapters, re-examine the attributes of your solution in terms of how they support your prospect's strategic goals.

5. Signaling criteria is a term coined by Michael Porter in *Competitive Advantage,* Free Press, 1985, p. 142.

Part 4

Selling

13

Selling the Benefit

Personally, I am always willing to learn, although I do not always like to be taught.

Winston Churchill

So far, the discussion in this book has centered around objective issues such as understanding your customer's business, finding ways to improve it, and quantifying the benefit of the product you offer. Although that's critical to success in selling complex business solutions, please do not get the idea that selling your benefit is merely a cold-blooded process of analyzing business and juggling numbers. Nothing could be further from the truth. If that were all it takes to succeed in selling complex systems, the accountants would be earning all the commission dollars.

Ultimately sales is not about financial analysis; it is about influencing people. A sale and purchase is a *social* transaction just as much as it is a *financial* transaction. Of course, you can't draw much water from a shallow well, so a strong financial justification can carry you a long way in your selling efforts. Think of your financial justification as the engine that drives your sales, but your sales skills are needed to steer your sales efforts in the right direction.

Salespeople are still needed and will always be needed because the buyer's decision-making process does not rest on logic alone. Logic is extremely important and can sometimes support emotional decisions, but subjective factors still play a large role in the buying decision, even in complex financial transactions. The science of economics has long assumed that people make rational decisions about their well-being, attempting to maximize economic utility in their decisions. However, some recent research has begun to study the "irrational" influences in decision making. Researchers are discovering what sales professionals have known for many years: subjective factors can creep into the rational, economic decision in many ways. The role of emotion and downright irrationality is far more prevalent than it would appear on the surface and is sometimes as important as the logical justification.

After all, the people to whom you are selling are still people, and their mastery of numbers and hard business data does not detract from that fact. This chapter discusses how to integrate your financial and business knowledge into a selling approach that satisfies the buyer's need for both logical justification and psychological support for the buying decision. First we will consider the various nonrational influences that affect buying decisions, then we'll see the role these influences play at the various stages of the sales cycle. Finally, we will discuss ways of dealing with these factors and turning them to our advantage.

NONRATIONAL INFLUENCES ON BUYING DECISIONS

Incomplete or Ambiguous Information

The most important reason for emotion to play a part in what should be a rational decision is incomplete information. Any investment is a forecast about the future, and no one can know with any certainty how the investment will work out. Will it work exactly as the salesperson says it will? Will it be installed in time? What new business conditions might arise that will cause actual results to deviate from expected results? When information is incomplete, risk increases, and when risk increases, emotional factors rise in prominence. Even when there is enough information to make an informed decision, buyers might be constrained by nagging doubts about the truth of what the salesperson has told them.

Information is also limited by time pressures. In a perfect world, every buyer would have unlimited time to gather all the necessary information, make valid comparisons between competing alternatives, and test assumptions to maximize the odds of making the right decision. Today's business environment does not permit that luxury. Opportunities to gain competitive advantage are fleeting at best, and those who take too long to decide may find that the window of opportunity has rapidly come and gone, especially with purchases of high-tech items.

The process of gathering information to make the correct decision is also constrained by cost. It takes money to employ people to analyze alternatives, shop for the best deal, negotiate with vendors, and so forth. There is also the opportunity cost of the benefits forgone during the time it takes to decide. Once it can be shown that your solution will bring measurable benefits and profit improvements to your customers, every day that they do not install your product is costing them money. An acquaintance of mine who sells energy-saving devices puts it this way: "You're already paying for my product; you just haven't installed it yet."

Sometimes the problem is not only incomplete information; your buyers might also be subject to misleading information (or at least think they are). There is always a competitor involved in every purchasing decision. Usually there is at least one competitor from outside the customer's company, but sometimes the competition is internal, or simply the decision to do nothing. The point is, there are others involved in the decision who have their own interests in mind, and they have an interest in putting forth their own points of view. (There is no need to impute dishonesty to them; they may have legitimate differences of opinion or perspective.) What may seem obvious to you becomes much more cloudy in the prospect's mind when the competition meets with that prospect. Your competitor will try to base the terms of the decision on the competitor's own strengths just as you will try to frame it around yours. If your competitor, for example, has a lower-priced product, it will naturally try to center the decision around short-term costs and downplay or ignore the benefits your product provides over the long term. This battle for the customer's mind share can turn just as easily on questions of personal credibility and "chemistry" as on numerical differences. Adding to the confusion is the fact that your competitors may have centers of influence within the account that differ from yours.

Personal Wins

This book has so far focused on business benefits, which implies that what is best for the business is the rational decision. However, every business decision is made by a real person who expects personal benefits from making the right decision, or—what may be more important—personal consequences from making the wrong decision. The salesperson must get to know the individuals involved in the decision and their personal hopes, aspirations, and fears. Complex, large-dollar sales typically involve many people in the decision-making process, and the personal issues of each must be addressed. Sometimes individual needs can even conflict with the business needs. As if the salesperson didn't have a difficult enough task just finding out personal issues, in such cases you must also tailor your sales effort to take into account individual differences in interests and needs. For example, a solution that gives service technicians the ability to complete more jobs in one day can be justified on the grounds of either increased service revenue, or reduced cost for the same level of revenue. As the old saying goes, where you stand on an issue depends on where you sit.

Personal Style

People do not all make decisions the same way. Some are orderly, methodical, and rational, while others are more intuitive or impulsive. An entire industry has formed around training salespeople to recognize and adjust for different buyer styles. Salespeople have learned that some buyers expect detailed analyses, backed by extensive data and evidence and presented in orderly spreadsheets. Others do not want to be bored by too much information but instead want the bottom line. Still others are much more likely to become fired up over the vision painted by the salesperson about how the product can improve their image, destroy the competition, or offer the latest and greatest technology.

Personal style also has another effect on the buying decision. In fact, some salespeople build their entire careers around this factor: people are much more likely to buy from you, or at least listen to you, if they like you. Even if you have the greatest product on the market, it will not help if you cannot get time on the prospect's calendar because he or she doesn't like your style.

Trust and Credibility

Your buyers must believe what you say. When people must make an important decision based on incomplete information, they tend to stick with the familiar, or the decision that is easiest to justify later. That is why a national reputation or brand name is so important in sales. If you work for such a company, your prospects probably accord you a higher level of credibility than they do your smaller competitors. If you work for one of the less-well-known firms, your task is necessarily more difficult. It is especially difficult today because of the natural tendency of those listening to us to resist what they are told, at least initially. Perhaps this is a legacy of the thousands of sales messages that bombard us daily, but telling someone how great your solution is seems to provoke an automatic reaction. As the quote at the beginning of the chapter implies, sometimes it is better to let buyers discover the truth for themselves.

EMOTION AND LOGIC IN THE SALES CYCLE

Think of the sales cycle as three phases: discovery of the problem, comparison of alternative solutions, and the decision phase. Every purchasing decision, when considered over the entire sales cycle, involves both emotion and logic, subjective as well as objective factors. Emotion plays a more important role at the discovery and the decision stages of the sales cycle, while logic carries greater weight during the comparison phase. Let us examine the impact of emotion at the beginning and the end of the sales cycle.

The Beginning of the Sales Cycle

At the beginning of the sales cycle, the principal emotional factors that will affect your success are trust and risk. Consider the frame of mind of your prospects at this phase: perhaps they have no idea that they have a business problem, so they might be skeptical at best about talking to someone who will try to convince them that they do. If you have not met your prospect personally, you will have to gain his or her trust before you can even begin to obtain the information you need to build your business case. The people to whom you are selling do not have an unlimited amount of time to devote to salespeople, and they guard it jealously. Add to that their natural suspicion of salespeople, and you have a daunting task ahead of you just to get in the door, much less to gain their trust and get them to open up about their personal and business aspirations; their challenges, problems, and fears; or the details of their proprietary business processes.

There are several ways to deal with the trust issue, although not all are under your personal control as a salesperson. For example, as noted, the reputation and size of your company, or the value of your brand, will play a very large role in establishing the initial atmosphere of trust and credibility. If you work for a large, well-established company, sometimes the mere mention of your company's name is enough to magically open doors for you. Some companies carry such large reputations in their particular industry that the business might be theirs to lose, rather than an uphill struggle to win. During its golden years IBM was a perfect example. Even today, IBM's reputation is such that it is automatically considered as one of the alternatives in many decisions, even when its salespeople are not initially involved.

At the other end of the spectrum, you may represent a relatively unknown company with an unproved technology or product line. In this case you may face a daunting task just to get your foot in the door and be noticed.

Another factor in gaining your prospect's trust, one over which you definitely have some control, is the initial impression you make on the prospect, either in your introductory correspondence or in your first sales call. In this case financial preparation can play a significant part, as your knowledge of the customer's business and industry will go a long way toward establishing your right to meet with high-level executives and ask them questions about their business.

Risk also plays a part in the early stages of the sales cycle, and you might be able to harness it to your advantage. Let's say you are selling a new technology that is not well known but that theoretically can offer significant business benefits to your customers. If they don't know too much about it, their strongest emotion might be mild interest. They certainly do not have a sense of urgency to change the status quo. Think about what you are asking your customers to do: to seriously consider changing a situation with which they might be totally comfortable, for unproved and uncertain benefit, and give a lot of money to a stranger. No wonder sales is so tough!

The way out of this difficult situation is to turn risk to your advantage. You have to shake your prospects out of their complacency and convince them that status quo is riskier than change. And you have to do it tactfully enough that they don't shoot the messenger—in fact, they thank you for bringing the matter to their attention. Later in this chapter we will see how this is done.

Another emotional factor you must consider is that the prospect also has to like you personally. Except when your product is so compelling that the customer has no choice, people tend to buy from people they like. Even when a dispassionate, logical consideration of all alternatives would clearly show your product to be superior, you might never get to that point if the prospect does not like you.

The End of the Sales Cycle

At the end of the sales cycle, risk comes back into play with a vengeance. During the beginning and middle stages of the process, the purchase decision is still off in the future. However, when it comes time to sign on the dotted line, the buyer is still taking a significant risk no matter how well you have built your case. Regardless of the amount of detail buyers have been able to amass on the potential benefits of the investment, their decisions are still based on projections about future conditions that may or may not actually arise. Often these projections are based on assumptions that may not hold up in real life, and large investments, in which you would expect that the most due diligence has taken place, are even riskier simply because of the magnitude of the dollars involved.

The buyer's mental state is affected by the possibility that, at the very least, the investment will not turn out to be as spectacular as envisioned. At worst, it could be a total flop, and reputation and even career could be at stake. At times like this, the "safe choice" is not necessarily the one with the highest projected internal rate of return;

it might be the one with the lowest chance of loss. People don't always try to make the best decision; frequently they try to make the least bad decision.

In fact, one of the earliest discoveries of the economists studying decision making under uncertainty is that, for the average person, losses loom much larger than gains. There are several reasons for this. For one, many buyers quite simply might not be able to afford the business or personal consequences of a wrong decision. If a company had earnings last year of one million dollars, earning an extra million dollars next year would be nice, but earning one million dollars less would be catastrophic. That is why we have an insurance industry. We are perfectly willing to pay a thousand dollars for car insurance (even if the law did not require it) to avoid a loss of $30,000, but how many of us would pay a thousand dollars for a lottery ticket with the same odds and same payoff? Additionally, the worse the potential consequences of an event, the more our minds tend to magnify the chances of its occurrence.

Because losses loom larger than gains, the salesperson has two courses of action available. First, you should reassure buyers that they are making the right decision. Detailed financial proposals backed by strong proofs such as testimonials, proof of concept, and benchmarking can go a long way toward alleviating a buyer's anxiety. They can also provide insurance by proving the buyer's due diligence in analyzing the decision. Second, you can sometimes use the risk in your favor. Turn the reason for buying from "Here's what you'll get if you buy it" to "Here's what you'll lose if you don't."

Dealing with risk may also be complicated by the personal style of the buyer. Individual buyers have different tolerances for risk and deal with risk in different ways. There are several well-known models of buyers' social and work styles, and most well-trained sales professionals are familiar with at least one.

OUTSIDE-IN SELLING

Dealing with the complex combination of business value and personal psychology requires a special approach to the sales process. In the Introduction, we talked about outside-in thinking, which is the mindset that drives you to think about the sales situation from the point of view of the customer. Putting this thought process into practice is outside-in selling. This chapter exposes you to some ideas that seem to run counter to accepted sales lore, or at least to the stereotypical view of salespeople characterized by Willy Loman in *Death of a Salesman.*

Salespeople who practice "inside-out selling" begin with their own issues, needs, and concerns (making quota this month, learning the features of new products, etc.) and project them onto their buyers. They talk about themselves, their companies, and their products and spend very little time questioning their customers to find out their issues. The buyer is an adversary who must be conquered or "won over" if the salesperson is to achieve his or her own goal.

Salespeople who know how to practice outside-in selling understand their customers' needs, issues, and challenges; they "get on the same side of the desk" as their customers. They take ownership of their customer's problems and work together with the customer to find a solution. Most important, just as the Socratic approach to teaching does not force the right answers on pupils but lets them find the right answers within themselves instead, outside-in salespeople lead their customers to discover the right choice.

Features, Benefits, and Needs

In Chapter 2 we visited the old FAB selling approach: Feature, Advantage, Benefit. It goes something like this: "Our deluxe widget comes with three-button control, as compared with the competition's two-button model, which allows you the flexibility to widgetize a wider variety of schmurples." This is a tried-and-true method that is very effective for giving inexperienced salespeople the basic tools to move widgets quickly.

The problem with the approach is that it is very inefficient. You might have to go through many features before you pile on enough benefits to outweigh your customer's resistance, and many of the benefits may be meaningless to that specific customer. Also, as we saw earlier, buyers will unconsciously resist what you tell them, even if it makes perfect logical sense.

Since you are reading this book, you have probably abandoned this style of selling, but a friendly reminder may be in order, if only to set a (negative) standard for comparison.

In outside-in selling, you turn the FAB approach around. You do not begin with features; you do not begin with advantages; you do not even begin with benefit. Instead, you begin with your customers' needs. Using your research, knowledge of your customers' business issues and processes, and your questions, you get customers to tell you what their real business and personal needs are. This is a joint process of discovery, because often you are not the only one discovering that there is a need. After you have established the need, together you work out the benefit, quantified if possible, of filling that need. Only then do you demonstrate the features that will help your prospects fill that need.

The surprising result of this style of selling is that many times your prospect does not even question your ability to supply those features to meet that need! The very process of joint discovery of business needs carries an implicit message to your buyer that you have a solution.

Other benefits to using the outside-in approach with your buyers include:

- Higher value—When you and the customer clearly establish the need up front, it elevates the value of the solution in the customer's mind. This makes it easier to justify the price you charge and makes negotiations easier.
- Urgency—Bringing out the full need will usually increase the level of pain associated with the problem, and the customer's willingness to do something about it will increase. This can shorten your sales cycle.
- Lower resistance —As you and the customer define the problem together, there is a shared sense of ownership in the solution that is offered. There is lower resistance because the customer helps you create the solution.
- Smoother relationships—When customers are "sold," there is generally a higher level of buyer's remorse, when the customer questions the decision that was made. This can make for rocky relationships. Consultative selling reduces the buyer's remorse because the customer feels better about the decision.
- Trust—This approach also builds up the level of trust between you and your customer, and you are seen as a valuable contributor to the customer's team. When you sell the customer the old-fashioned way, you are constantly having to prove yourself.

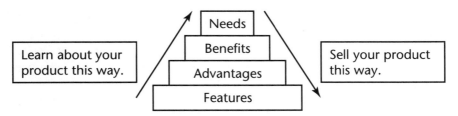

Figure 13-1. The Needs Pyramid

The FAB model does have its place in selling, if only to learn about your product. If your company introduces a new product, the marketing team will probably tell you first about the features that make it different and the advantages that those features carry over the old product. Your next step is to figure out what the benefits of these new features are for your buyers. Think of the process as steps in a pyramid, as shown in Figure 13-1.

Defining the Need

Although the needs pyramid may look simple to formulate for a specific sales opportunity, the real art of selling is in defining the need to be filled. Selling a "solution" implies that you and the buyer both have a clear understanding of and agreement on the problem. This is not as easy as it sounds, but it is critical to an effective sales process. You must discover, and in come cases influence, the buyer's compelling reason to buy your product. In fact, defining the need is the central prerequisite of any successful sales effort.

Although that may sound obvious, it is very common to see sales opportunities in which the salesperson has lost sight of the real reason the buyer might want the product. Partly this is a result of the "inside-out" mentality which is natural for salespeople under quota. You know why you want to sell the product, but have you really thought long and hard about why the customer might actually want to buy it? Another reason that salespeople may not think about the customer's needs enough is that they are afraid to ask themselves the hard questions. The problem is that if you gloss over the fact that the customer does not have a real compelling need to buy, you will eventually find out—but only after you have spent a lot of time and money in the sales process.

If you have ever been frustrated by a sales opportunity that just seems to drag on, where the benefits of the product were obvious to you but the buyer did not seem to be in a hurry to make a decision, or you had trouble getting to the right people in the organization, you may have failed to properly define the real need to be filled.

Unless the customer has a compelling problem, your own need to sell will not stand much of a chance of being fulfilled. The fact is, investments of money by customers do not exist in a vacuum, particularly with higher-ticket items. This has always been true and is even more so today, but the majority of salespeople ignore it.

The need is the motivating reason and therefore the central convincing argument around which your sale is built. At the same time, cultivating the habit of focusing on the customer's true need is the foundation upon which enduring relationships rest. The need can be personal or business in nature, and it will also vary from individual to individual within the same organization, even for the same sales opportunity.

In business, needs exist because the existing situation is somehow causing a problem for your customer. Usually it's because the company has someplace it wants to go and it "can't get there from here," or the existing situation somehow presents obstacles to the attainment of corporate goal. This destination could be a specified business goal or a vision of the future that managers are trying to achieve. The problem might also exist because some new situation has arisen that threatens the company's maintenance of the status quo. It could be a competitor with a new product, changing demands from the market, or just about anything else. Because the problem is impairing the company's ability to meet specified business goals, the financial cost of the problem can often be measured.

Of course, the true need is not always explicit or obvious at first glance. And, it is *not* always driven by the customer. In fact, listening too closely to what the customer says he or she needs can often be a prescription for failure. Remember, your customers may be experts in their business operations and in the problems confronting them, but they are not necessarily experts in the solutions available. At the same time, the rapid pace of change in business today ensures that many of the problems your customers face are presenting themselves for the first time. Finally, customer-defined needs are frequently framed by what the customer considers possible or feasible, but you may offer a technology that is so new or different that the customer has no idea of what is possible.

Frequently your biggest competitor is not another company delivering a similar product, but rather your customers' established ways of doing things. Sometimes customers do not know what they want until they know it is possible, then they can't live without it. If customers always defined their own needs, the world never would have seen spreadsheet software, fax machines, pet rocks, or Federal Express.

DEALING WITH THE EMOTIONAL FACTOR

The principal tool for addressing the emotional component of the buyer's decision is a well-considered list of questions. Your ultimate goal in dealing with your customers' subjective decision-making process is to *get your customers to tell you what you want them to hear.* Go back and read that sentence again. We are so accustomed to being bombarded with thousands of sales messages every day that our natural defense mechanism is to be very skeptical of anything anyone tells us. Even when we accept the truth of what people tell us, we may feel a bit like "shooting the messenger." The way to get around this natural tendency is to refrain from telling your customers that they need your product. Instead, help your customers to *tell you* they need your product. This is certainly not a new idea; teachers have been using it for years, since a fellow called Socrates used it in the Athens school almost 2,500 years ago. However, it can be difficult for salespeople to accept. We are so accustomed to making presentations and influencing people by talking to them, that it seems counterintuitive to suppose that we can actually have more influence by *asking* and *listening* than by *telling.* And again, many of us learned how to sell in the old feature-advantage-benefit school, where it seems that efficiency in listing the benefits of our product was more prized than taking the time to find out the customer's needs.

Well-crafted questions can be used to guide your customers in a joint discovery process, by which you and the customer together arrive at the right decision. Properly done, the process can help your customers discover for themselves that they have a problem, quantify the impact the problem has on them and their business, and conclude that your product is the right solution. Effective questioning is an art form which has been best described in *SPIN Selling* (McGraw-Hill, 1998) by Neil Rackham. It is not an easy process to master and certainly cannot be done when "winging it" on a sales call. You must begin with a clear idea of the need to be filled and then craft your questions to lead your customer to it.

14

Talking to the Right People

The new regional president had a problem. George had just accepted the promotion to president of one of the company's smaller regions. That was the good news. The bad news was that the region he had just taken over was the perennial last-place finisher out of eight—measured by profitability, revenue growth, and customer complaints, to name just a few. The region would not have been his first choice, but George saw it as an opportunity to make a name for himself if he could turn it around. Success here could mean a boost toward his personal goal of rising to the top of the company's management ranks.

But first he had to get a grip on the problems of his own patch of the company. While dreams of eventual corporate leadership were compelling, he had more immediate worries. In the high-stakes game of corporate politics, he knew that if he could not turn it around in a reasonable time, he could lose his job. With one child entering college that fall and another just a year away, he could not afford to fail.

George spent the first few weeks analyzing the region's performance and prioritizing the needs he saw. Although several avenues of improvement presented themselves, he lighted on what he viewed as the most immediate need: improving the level of customer service. His region had a much higher "churn" level than the others. Although the sales force was doing a decent job of adding new customers, too many of these customers were leaving in the first year. It cost a lot of money to add a new subscriber to the company's service, and the average subscriber had to remain a customer for at least 10 months before the cost of acquisition was recouped and the company began to make any money. The president got his financial officer to run some figures, and he found that, if he could just reduce churn to the average of all the other regions, he could add approximately $2 million to quarterly earnings. That would be a great way to begin his tenure, and none of the other problems appeared as serious compared with the churn issue.

He had his marketing staff investigate the reasons for such a high defection rate, but being a hands-on manager, he also followed his own hunch. Posing as a customer, he called the customer service line and found that he was put on hold for as long as several minutes before anybody could come to his assistance. He was not surprised when his marketing department reported back that the number-one reason given by customers for switching service was the difficulty in figuring out the monthly bills and the frustration they felt when they tried to call the company help line for assistance.

Next he turned to the Director of Customer Service to find out why there was such a long delay in processing requests for information. She told him that she was aware of the problem, and that was why she had requested a 20 percent head-count increase in the past two budgets, but she had been rebuffed each time. George said he would approve the increase if that was what it took to solve the problem, but he knew it would not be an easy sell back at corporate HQ, so he wanted to be absolutely sure that was the only alternative.

At his previous region, he had seen a similar problem and had initially tried to address it through training. Although they saw some improvement, they found that the main reason for delays was the difficulty in finding and accessing customer billing and service records. When a customer called with a question or complaint, it was necessary to have a lot of information available in order to track down the problem and create a solution. Either the information was stored in separate computer systems, each of which had to be accessed separately, or it had to be dug out of paper archives, all of which combined to create long delays, which frustrated customers waiting on the line. Some of these customers switched to the competitor in hopes of receiving better service. Others were bound by contracts but switched as soon as they had the opportunity. Although the marketing study did not ask the question, George was also sure that they were telling their friends about the poor service, which was making it harder for the sales force to win business.

NAVIGATING THE DECISION-MAKING PROCESS

What does this story tell us about navigating the decision-making process in a complex sale? Several things: it shows that a sale to a corporation can involve many different people and demonstrates how the business problem to be solved differs depending on the position of the person; it points out the importance of calling at high levels in the prospect's organization; and it offers clues for using a business problem-solving approach to gain access at different levels in the decision-making process. Let's examine each lesson in greater detail.

Positions in the Decision-Making Process

Solution sales to companies that require a large investment are usually a cooperative decision, involving many people at various levels and representing different departments. The number of people involved, their positions, their amount of interest in the decision, and their influence will all vary from decision to decision. Because the decision-making process requires an ad hoc grouping of individuals to solve a specific problem, it will reflect not only the formal but also the informal levels of power and influence in the organization. Therefore it is possible to have lower-ranking individuals with more power in the decision than their immediate superiors.

There is a potentially limitless number of combinations, but most decisions will involve the following players. (Not every decision will necessarily involve all these roles, especially the smaller ones. Sometimes a single individual assumes more than one role simultaneously. If the project is already budgeted, for example, the key decision maker could also be the approver.)

Key Decision Maker

Although large investment decisions are usually joint decisions, sometimes even involving buying committees, there is usually one individual who, either by appointment or by reasons of position, personal interest, personal expertise, or simple force of personality, will have the lion's share of the influence in the decision. This is the most important person in your sales process, and a significant portion of your sales strategy must be centered around gaining influence with this individual. In our example, George is the key decision maker, by virtue of both his position and his strong interest in driving the project to completion. His principal business interest in the investment decision is financial results.

However, do not automatically assume that the person with the highest position is the key decision maker. High-level executives may assign someone else the task of making the decision because they do not have the time or expertise to evaluate alternatives and meet with vendors.

Approver

The approver is the person who has the final say in whether the purchase will go through. The approver is like Congress: the president may decide, but Congress controls the purse strings, so nothing will happen without its approval. In our example, George decides to go through with the project and may choose the vendor, but no money will be spent unless headquarters releases the funds. Their interest in the decision is usually based on financial justification, so they will be a principal target of your financial proposal. Approvers may have little or a lot of say in the process, depending on the situation. Some simply "rubber-stamp" the KDM's decision, although others may take a very active role in the process.

Recommenders

Clearly there are many other people in the organization who will be affected by the final decision. Either out of personal interest or technical or financial expertise, they will either make recommendations to the key decision maker or influence the decision in other ways. The Vice President of Marketing, for instance, has an interest in operational performance, in the form of lower churn and higher market share. The Director of Customer Service is concerned with operational performance in the form of reduced waiting time for customers calling in, and also with personnel issues such as training, acceptance of the new system by the staff, and ease of use. The Chief Financial Officer was initially drawn into the situation because of the interest in improving profitability, but he gradually realized that improving the process of resolving billing issues could significantly improve accounts receivable collection, which might bring in a lot of cash initially and help defray the initial investment. The Information Technology Director was concerned that any IT solution should integrate smoothly with existing systems and should function to the advertised technical specifications.

Problem Owner

In financial selling, it is critical to define the customer's problem correctly and then identify the individual responsible for the consequences of solving or not solving it. The way you define the problem will have a significant impact on the perceived value of the solution, the customer's sense of urgency in solving the problem, and your level of influence in the organization.

Identifying the Problem Owner

In financial selling, the problem owner is defined as the person responsible for the underlying business problem. It is not necessarily the person tasked with solving the problem; it is the person who stands to gain the most if the problem is solved—or to lose the most if it is not. Who owns the problem in this example? Depending on how the problem is defined, it could actually be one person or several people in the organization.

Business problems typically have three dimensions: financial, operational, and technical. Think of each of these dimensions as the answer to the following three questions: Why? What? and How?

- Why is this being done?—What are the expected financial results that will occur if the problem is solved?
- What must be done?—What changes must be made to our operations or processes in order to yield the financial results?
- How will it be done?—What is technically the most efficient way of implementing a solution that will deliver the performance we need, with minimum disruption and risk, and as quickly as possible?

Because there are three dimensions to the problem, complex sales opportunities may comprise three different levels of problem owners: financial, operational, and technical. The financial problem owner is responsible for bottom-line results, the operational problem owner wants to see measurable business process improvements, and the technical problem owner is tasked with making the new solution work quickly and properly.

If the problem has already been defined as a customer service issue and the solution has already been identified as a document-imaging system, then the problem owner would seem to be the person in IT tasked with selecting and implementing the best technical solution. If one has not already been installed, maybe an imaging system is the last thing he would want. Why disrupt his routine just to install another "bleeding-edge" technology that will monopolize his time and create even more headaches than he already has? He has enough trouble keeping up with existing systems and answering stupid questions from ignorant users. Because it is this person's job to implement the system, a lot can be gained or lost from the eventual outcome. Suppose it takes too long to implement, or does not work right when it is implemented. Or what if it disrupts the existing IT architecture? Who loses then? His success or failure is measured in terms of time and functionality of the hardware and software, and user satisfaction.

Clearly another problem owner is the manager of the Customer Service department. She has an operational problem: she must reduce waiting time on the telephone from several minutes to several seconds. Probably her job is on the line if these standards are not met; certainly her bonus and career prospects will be affected. Her critical measurement of success is waiting time.

What about the VP of Marketing? She owns a business problem. Her mission is to reduce churn by two percentage points. She faces the same potential consequences and rewards as the Director of Customer Service. Of course, even before George got there, she faced this problem and tried different ways to deal with it, but now the problem is even more urgent. It has been elevated from one of several problems to the highest priority. Her critical measurement is churn, or customer turnover.

The Chief Financial Officer also owns a business problem. He is very interested in reducing churn, but his most important measure is profit. Maybe he will not lose his job if the problem is not solved, because he has no direct responsibility for it, but his bonus may be affected. Plus, he knows that being associated with the lowest-ranking region in the company is not the surest route to advancement.

George wants profits to rise, but his ultimate measure of success is his area's ranking among the various regions. This project is just one of several different strategies and initiatives to get to his goal of the number-one ranking, but it has one of the highest priorities.

Each of these individuals is involved somehow in the decision-making process. Although they are all working toward a common goal, each has a different perspective on the problem. They all measure success or failure differently, so each is looking for something a little different out of this transaction. The salesperson attempting to navigate this process must keep these differences in mind and adapt the approach to each person according to the individual's specific concerns.

With all these potential problem definitions, which one should the salesperson concentrate on? The answer depends on your personal expertise and the strengths of your solution versus competing alternatives. All things being equal, it makes sense to attack the financial problem, which is theoretically the ultimate reason that any business decisions are made. However, from a strategic standpoint, the best chance you have to win the business is to go with your strengths or attack the competitor's weaknesses. If you can credibly discuss the financial ramifications of your solution and can show how your solution directly addresses the financial issues, then by all means build your approach around the financial problem owner. If your principal strength is technical, then you should attack the technical problem and build bridges with the technical problem owners. Of course, you should, within the constraints of the time and resources available, cast as wide a net as possible in your search for problem owners. You can never have too many friends in the customer's company, especially since your competitor is attempting the same thing.

Calling High

Although you must build relationships at various levels in order to have a successful sale, there are many reasons for calling at the highest level possible within the customer's organization.

The View Is Better at the Top

Prior to George's arrival in the region, other imaging sales reps had called on the same account, with little success. The typical response seemed to be: "Interesting technology, but we don't really need it, and anyway we can't afford it." The need was always there, but nobody had taken a broad enough look at the problem. Each of the people contacted had a limited view of the organization's problems; like the fabled blind men feeling the elephant, they all had their own limited perspectives of what was needed. In this case the problem was much bigger than any one department, and it took a person at a high enough level to see the forest instead of the trees. Depending on the magnitude, cost, and impact of your product, sometimes the only person who can see the strategic benefit you bring to the organization is at the highest levels of management. While the economic justification was essential to getting the project approved, it was also critical that the project would help the regional president meet his personal goals within the organization.

At the same time, only George and possibly the Chief Financial Officer knew enough about the strategic priorities of the region to compare this investment opportunity against others. The way the problem was defined meant that it was no longer a document-imaging problem: it was a customer-retention problem. George might have decided instead to attack the problem through more advertising dollars, or better training of customer service personnel. Forewarned by talking to the regional president, the salesperson could concentrate on customer retention instead of operating efficiencies, for example. Working only at lower levels, the salesperson could have put together an "airtight" cost justification against other imaging solutions—and still have been totally off the mark.

Buying Authority

Everybody involved had personal goals related to this acquisition, but only George had the authority and, probably more important, the confidence to approve spending such a large sum to solve the problem. Even if lower-level influencers in the decision-making process saw the need and were championing the purchase through the organization, the decision eventually had to come to George for approval. Why not start with him early in the process?

Speed

At higher levels, executives make a lot of important and expensive decisions; that's their job. A large investment, while not to be taken lightly, is just another one of many important decisions they make every day, so they will usually decide quickly when they are convinced they have enough information. Additionally, since they are less likely to have someone second-guessing their decisions, you won't have to deal as much with requirements designed primarily to cover the recommender's tracks in case the investment does not work out. At lower levels, every decision is proportionally larger, so the buyers will require much more from the seller before deciding.

Common Sense

Of all these reasons, probably the most important is that almost anybody in the decision-making process can say "no," but there is only one person who can say "yes."

A disclaimer on calling high: Regardless of the strong reasons for calling high in the prospect's organization, you must not use that as your only strategy. You must also develop relationships and sell at the other levels in the company, or you run the risk of winning the battle and losing the war. Salespeople who step on the backs of lower-level influencers, or ignore them, often find to their dismay that they get no help when it comes time to make the product work. After the product is sold, it still must be implemented properly within the organization in order for it to work as advertised.

Gaining Access

In this example the decision to purchase was driven from the top, because George had previously purchased a similar system and had a clear idea of what he needed to solve his business problem. But suppose that had not been the case. If you were selling a similar system, and you decided to approach the company for the first time, how would you do it?

Since you know that there are many advantages to calling high and driving the sale from the top, you decide to begin your sales effort with George. But how do you get time on his calendar to see him? He has just taken over a new region and clearly has a lot competing for his attention. Probably the last thing he wants to do is talk to a salesperson.

There are several approaches you can take to get an audience with the high-level executive. They do not always work, but they do increase your odds of success. However, there is one approach guaranteed not to work: call him and ask him if you can meet with him to discuss the latest imaging technology. *(Insert your own product description here.)* Remember, George is not interested in imaging technology. He is interested in increasing profits and climbing to number one. If you come in talking technology, and features, and functionality, it will be like speaking a different language. When you are talking to high-level executives, product comes last. It is only a means to an end. You are not selling product; you are selling profits. It would be like a travel agent trying to sell you a vacation package to an exotic resort by describing the technical features of the airplane that will take you there. You are not selling transportation; you are selling a destination. While George is not likely to spare time to talk to someone about imaging systems, he will probably be interested in talking to a consultant who can show him how to reduce churn and increase profits.

If you want to gain access to top executives, you must earn the right. You can do this only by building your approach in the language they speak daily. That means being prepared to discuss their business issues and ask targeted questions that add to knowledge you already have. They will not want to waste time educating you, but they will answer intelligent questions that demonstrate expertise and preparation. You must also be able to show them very quickly that you understand their problems and have a solution that will not only solve the problems but also deliver the results they seek according to the measurements they value.

Actually, that last paragraph applies to *anybody* to whom you are trying to gain access. Know what people are looking for, and how they will measure success. If you know that, that is what you are selling. In our example, sell *profits* and *customer retention*, not imaging technology. In other words, sell the ends, not the means.

When you know what your prospect is looking for, you can devise a *value proposition* which succinctly defines the need and the solution you bring that fills that need. Properly done, a value proposition piques the prospect's interest and demonstrates personal credibility. This value proposition will be the central element of your approach to the prospect. Use it in your initial correspondence or telephone approach.

Going through the exercise of writing a value proposition can be a valuable experience in itself, because you cannot prepare a good one unless you know a lot. It will force you to think hard about the customer, and to make the connection between your product and the company's success. If you cannot think of a reasonably powerful or credible value proposition, then you should back off and think a bit more before you waste your only opportunity with this executive.

Obviously this approach requires some preparation. You will never succeed making a "cold call" to a high-level executive. The downside to calling at the top is that you usually get only one chance to do it right, this is a rifle-shot approach which must be handled with care. Make sure you know as much as possible about the customer's business goals and challenges the company faces, and be prepared to demonstrate knowledge of the industry. The next chapter will give you pointers on preparing and executing the high-level sales call.

OVERCOMING "LEVEL LOCK"

In some cases, you may already have a relationship established with a lower-level influencer, or you may have been contacted by someone to enter a bid. Although you know the value of calling high, you are concerned that going over that person's head will harm your chances of winning any business.

While a number of sales strategies can be effective in this situation, let us just look at how the bottom-line selling approach can be employed:

- Preempt—The best way to avoid level lock is to begin your initial approach at the proper levels. This will not help you with existing accounts, but you have a golden opportunity to "train" your new customers in how they should expect to be sold to.
- Raise the bar—Often the very process of your asking business and financial questions will communicate that the prospect is in over his or her head and must bring others into the evaluation process. Make sure that you offer to include this individual in future discussions. Your initial contact person must be convinced that granting access to others is not a threat to him or her personally but rather will help you design the best possible solution.

- Team up—If you are stuck at a technical level, bring in financial and operational experts to meet with the other problem owners.

FINDING A CHAMPION

The story also points out another lesson: It is helpful to have an advocate inside the customer's organization who is waving your flag when you are not there. The opportunity in this situation seems pretty clear, but in real life it could be difficult for the salesperson to discover that much about the problem, internal politics, and the needs of the different influencers. The surest way to shortcut a lot of the information gathering is to have a champion from inside the corporation who has a vested interest in seeing you succeed, and who is placed high enough in the organization to make a real difference.

People usually do not become your advocates just because they like you. They ally themselves with you because they see you as an avenue for solving a business problem faced by them personally or by their company. Usually the best way to find a champion is to identify the principal problem owner within the corporation and demonstrate your ability to make the problem go away.

While you are busy searching for a champion for your solution, don't forget to think defensively. Remember that your competitor might also have a champion or potential champion. Always try to think of who within the corporation stands to lose the most if your solution goes through. It may be an internal competitor who wants to "build an empire" by cornering internal resources to solve the problem himself, or a technical expert who has a vested interest in keeping the corporation on a standard in which she is best qualified. In some cases there may even be people whose jobs would go away if your solution is implemented. These will be particularly difficult to win over, to put it mildly; your best bet is to solidify your influence at the highest levels possible.

15

Developing Financial Proposals

Following the bottom-line selling process, you have no doubt spent a lot of time with different people in the customer's organization, gathering information, discussing options, and designing solutions that will deliver a measurable business impact. It is time to bring that information together in the form of a financial proposal which lays out the client's projected return on investment in a clear, easy-to-follow format. In its simplest sense, the proposal summarizes the expected outlay of funds, lists the projected benefits, and applies specific financial formulas in order to express the return in standard financial language—but it is really more than that.

THE PROPOSAL AS A SELLING TOOL

Although the proposal is where you will summarize the business motive for purchasing your product, never forget that it is more than a financial document; it is a selling tool which can work for you even when you are not physically in front of the customer.

The business decision makers to whom you are selling must make many investment decisions in the course of a year and—having limited funds at their disposal—must be choosy about where they put their money. The choice can be difficult because there are usually several alternatives, and the benefits of each may be expressed differently, making direct comparisons problematical. This confusion only adds to the existing element of risk and uncertainty, so your customer will appreciate the clarity and reassurance of a proper proposal. If it is well written, your financial proposal can lower the decision maker's actual and perceived risk in the decision.

Your customers are painfully aware that a single poor decision can undo a previous string of good ones, but they may lower their *personal risk* by making the decision defensible at a future date if necessary. In the event that the investment does not deliver as promised, the decision maker will be able to show that the choice was based on the best available information at the time, in accordance with accepted analytical processes. The proposal can also go a long way toward lowering *perceived risk* in the decision. As with any uncertain choice, more information will help make your numbers more credible. The depth of thought and detail that goes into the proposal will make a strong impression on the decision maker, so make sure the impression is positive.

We have already seen that purchasing decisions usually depend on both objective and subjective factors. A well-done proposal appeals to both those elements of the buyer's mind by sending the following messages:

- You have put a lot of thought into this investment opportunity.
- You understand the company's business issues.
- You are a consultative sales professional.
- There are quantifiable benefits to making this investment.

WHEN TO USE A FINANCIAL PROPOSAL— AND NOT

If your customer's procedures require a formal justification of the investment decision (especially common for large investments), your choice of whether or not to prepare a financial proposal is already made. Frequently, however, you have discretion in the matter, and the situation will dictate the best course of action. There are some sales situations in which using a financial proposal is a good idea, even if the customer does not require it:

- You are not the lowest-cost choice.—If the customer perceives competing alternatives as the same, the lowest cost will always win. Your proposal can be used to reinforce the differences between your solution and others, and quantify what that difference means to your customer.

- Funds have not yet been budgeted for this purchase.—This situation happens more often than you might think. In fact, if you have truly been an effective business consultant for your customer, you may have discovered needs that the company did not know it had; naturally there would not be funds available in the budget to solve these problems. The proposal can make the case that this investment provides a higher return than those that have already been included in the budget.
- The buyer's financial staff will get involved in the decision.— Proposals are the stock-in-trade of the financial types in your customer's company. If they feel out of their depth in evaluating technical merit, they will welcome the opportunity to work with a document they can understand.
- The decision maker needs the proposal to justify the decision.— Sometimes decision makers know exactly what they want but need a document to demonstrate that they have followed a coherent analytical process to make the decision.
- The proposal can be an intangible differentiator.—As mentioned, the proposal says a lot about your preparation, knowledge, and professionalism. Given two alternatives that on balance appear equal, your proposal might be the difference that wins the sale.

There are also times when it is not a good idea to develop a financial proposal for your customer:

- The decision maker and the approver have already agreed to proceed.—There is an old bit of sales lore that says you should never talk past the close, lest you give the buyer a reason to change his or her mind. If you already have an agreement to buy, and the people you are dealing with have the authority, you have everything to lose and nothing to gain by preparing a proposal. If they do not have the authority, you will have to use your judgment on whether or not to develop a proposal.
- You have not gained agreement on the value of your benefits.— The proposal is only as believable as the numbers that go into it.

If your buyers do not agree with your numbers, no amount of fancy financial formulation will convince them that your proposal has any merit. As they say, "Garbage in, garbage out." The proposal is the easy part; the hard part is getting agreement on the numbers to go into it. That is what makes this process *financial selling* instead of *financial analysis*.

- You do not have proof of your benefits.—The more evidence you have in the form of pilot or beta test results, or previous customers, the better off you are. Nevertheless, sometimes the only "proof" you have is that other people in the organization have agreed to your numbers. Since they are experts in those processes that you affect, their opinions will carry a lot of weight at executive levels. (If you don't have any of these to back you up, it's time to go back to the drawing board.)
- There is a chance your proposal will be shown to the competition.—Sometimes buyers will ask for proposals just to have evidence in their files that they considered other alternatives, when in fact they had already made the purchase decision long before and never had an intention of buying from you. In effect, your valuable time has been used to divulge sensitive information to your competitor. It's impossible to avoid this situation altogether, but proper qualification and your experience and judgment as a sales professional can help.

DOS AND DON'TS OF PROPOSALS

Keep in mind that your proposal represents you and your company. The following tips will help you to make a good impression.

- Use the outside-in selling approach: talk about them and their issues more than about your product.
- Know your audience: try to find out who will evaluate your proposal, and write it with them in mind, adjusting for their personal style, or interests within the corporation.
- Do not fill the document with technical jargon, unless it is exclusively for technical decision makers (in which case it's really not a financial proposal).
- Above all, do not pad the proposal with pages of information about your own company. That is the surest way to send the

impression that you are not focused on your customer. If you think decision makers are concerned with your ability to deliver, you may include information that specifically targets that issue.

ELEMENTS OF THE PROPOSAL

The length and amount of detail of your proposal will vary with the dollar amount of the investment, the complexity of the solution, and of course your customer's requirements. The full text can range from one page to an entire volume. However, all proposals should contain the following components:

- A restatement of the business problem—The solution you are selling exists only because a business problem exists. By restating the problem, you can reemphasize its importance; this will be especially helpful when others who have not been heavily involved review the proposal. It impresses on the reader that you clearly understand the business issues as well as the technical merits of your solution. Your restatement of the business problem can also be a good way to grab a reader's attention and make him want to read on.
- A brief description of your solution—Often the contents of this section will be dictated by your customer, as outlined in the company's request for proposal. You may be able to use this section to help lower the perceived risk of the solution, especially if your customer's likely questions are anticipated and answered. Don't leave out essential information, especially about the features that differentiate your solution, but keep this section as brief as possible.
- Presentation of your financial benefits—This is the core of the proposal. That is what the rest of this chapter is about.

THE FINANCIAL SECTION

Every investment is a dynamic calculation that balances three factors: cost, benefit, and risk. There are trade-offs among them, and the exact combination of each will depend on the needs and preferences of your buyer. The most commonly known is the traditional risk-reward trade: the greater the risk, the higher the potential reward, and vice versa. But cost is also important. In some cases higher initial cost may be justified in order to reap higher benefits, or to lower the risk involved. For example, when you purchase a service plan for that expensive stereo system, you have agreed to a higher cost in exchange for lower risk. But not everbody buys the service plan. The choice depends on the individual decision maker, and the potential combinations are endless. Hopefully, by the time you get to the point of preparing a financial proposal for your customer, you have a reasonable idea of the parameters of each element for that particular buyer.

Components of the Financial Section

A complete financial section in your proposal contains seven parts for which you will need to assemble information:

- Differential earnings projections—These are the additional cash inflows your customer can expect as a result of investing in your solution. It is not the additional expected profit, because profit, which is an accounting term, does not always match the cash that actually flows back into the company. The discussion of depreciation in the following section will help explain this concept.

  If your solution helps your customer reduce expenses, use the amount of expense reduction. However, if your solution helps the customer increase revenues, don't use the entire amount of increased revenues; use the expected increase in gross profit. If your solution contributes several benefits, list each separately. Be conservative—use the lower range of estimated benefits.
- Amount of the investment—Include the purchase price plus any additional expenses that may be required to implement the solution. Your buyers will take a close look at this figure, so don't try to fudge by leaving out these additional expenses. Also include any periodic expenditures that will need to be made over the life of the asset to keep it working, such as maintenance and service.
- Life of the asset—You and your customer must agree on the expected useful life of the asset. This figure will be needed to

compute the total lifetime benefits and to calculate depreciation for tax purposes. If you are not sure how long the asset may last, use the standard schedules approved by the IRS.

- Salvage and disposal value—This is an estimate of the future amount to be realized from selling or disposing of the asset at the end of its useful life. It is used both to calculate the total benefit and to compute depreciation for tax purposes.
- The customer's cost of capital—You will need this number to use some of the more sophisticated discounted cash flow techniques, which are explained later in this chapter.
- The customer's tax rate—You will need this to calculate the benefit from depreciation.
- Consideration of risk—Riskier investments require higher expected returns.

The Cash Flow Projection Worksheet

Up to this point, you have collected a large amount of information. To make it meaningful for you and easy to follow, put the data in a worksheet similar to the example shown in Figure 15-1.

Pay attention to the following points regarding the example:

1. The initial investment is based on the purchase price plus the additional cost to get the solution implemented. In this simple case, there is a charge of $50,000 to get the operators trained to run it properly. You will notice that the initial investment is considered being made in "year 0." The money will have to be spent up front in order to achieve the expected benefits in future years.

2. Expected benefits are calculated beginning with year 1. In many cases the first year's benefit will not be as high as ensuing years, because there might be a lag between initial installation of the asset and realization of maximum productivity, due to learning curves, working out bugs, meshing with other company processes, and so forth.

3. Deduct any ongoing expenses necessary to keep the asset in working condition.

Year	0	1	2	3	4	5
Investment						
Purchase Price	$200,000					
Salvage Value						50,000
Initial Training	50,000					
Total Investment	250,000	0	0	0	0	50,000
Benefits						
Benefit		$175,000	$200,000	$200,000	$220,000	$220,000
Benefit		15,000	15,000	15,000	15,000	15,000
Benefit						
Benefit						
Total Annual Benefit	0	190,000	215,000	215,000	235,000	235,000
Ongoing Costs						
Annual Maintenance		$25,000	$25,000	$25,000	$25,000	$25,000
Depreciation		30,000	30,000	30,000	30,000	30,000
Profit Before Tax		135,000	160,000	160,000	180,000	180,000
Taxes		45,900	54,400	54,400	61,200	61,200
Cash Flow						
Net Profit		$89,100	$105,600	$105,600	$118,800	$118,800
Plus: Depreciation		30,000	30,000	30,000	30,000	30,000
Plus: Salvage Value		0	0	0	0	50,000
Total Annual Cash Flow	−250,000	119,100	135,600	135,600	148,800	198,800
Cost of Capital	10					
Tax Rate	34					
Payback						
1.6 years						
Lifetime ROI						
195%						
Net Present Value						
$270,262.45						
Internal Rate of Return						
46%						

Figure 15-1.   Cash Flow Projection Worksheet

4. Depreciation expense involves a little accounting trickery. Depreciation is known as a noncash expense. It does not involve an actual cash outlay, but it can be deducted from profits for tax purposes. The solution is to include it in the annual

ongoing expenses in order to calculate profit before tax, and then deduct taxes from that figure; then, you can add back the total amount of depreciation to net profit to arrive at the total cash flow for that year. To figure out the annual depreciation expense, deduct the expected salvage value from the initial investment, and divide the difference by the expected useful life.

5. You can either get the company's tax rate by asking your contact, or use last year's actual tax rate from the company's annual report.

6. At the end of the useful life, salvage value is added back.

7. Cost of capital may obtained by asking the company. There are a number of sophisticated techniques you can use to calculate it yourself, but it is difficult to get a definitive answer, so your best bet is to get agreement from one of your customer's financial people.

Cash Flow Evaluation Techniques

The annual cash flow figures you computed and collated on the cash flow projection worksheet can now be used as the raw material to input into one or more of the various financial evaluation techniques used by your buyers. Today's firms use a variety of financial formulas to gauge the value of their investments. You will usually need to compute more than one, because there are advantages and disadvantages to each. The discussion that follows is not exhaustive, because there may be as many techniques as there are firms. Make sure you know which techniques are favored or required by your customers.

Payback

Payback is the oldest, simplest, and probably most commonly used method. Payback is expressed in terms of time. Quite simply, payback measures how much time it will take the firm to recoup its investment. Do not make the common mistake of saying things like, "Your payback is 20 percent," or "Your payback is $150,000."

For a regular cash flow stream, simply divide the initial investment by the expected annual (or monthly) return:

$$\text{Payback} = \frac{\text{Initial Investment}}{\text{Annual Benefit}}$$

For an irregular payment stream, the calculation is slightly more involved, although it is really common sense. The following example will show you how it is done:

Initial investment: **$200,000**
Year 1 cash flow: 45,000
Year 2 cash flow: 60,000
Year 3 cash flow: 75,000
Year 4 cash flow: 75,000

Add up the benefits one year at a time until you exceed the value of the initial investment. In this case, you must add all four years together. Since the total for all four years is $255,000, you know that the payback period is shorter than four years but longer than three. After three years, the cumulative benefit is $180,000. The remaining $20,000 is returned in approximately three months, because 20,000 divided by 75,000 equals .27 years.

The principal benefit of using payback is that it is so easy to calculate that it is almost intuitive. That is why almost everybody uses it at least as an initial estimate of the value of an investment, in order to weed out various alternatives or to decide whether to proceed further. Payback is also helpful in dealing with risk, because short payback periods minimize the risk of the investment.

The disadvantages of using payback as a financial measurement are that it makes no distinction between investments of different amounts, and it says nothing about the benefits that may accrue after the payback period. An investment may be slower to pay off but yield much greater benefits over the entire life of the asset. Because of this shortcoming, payback tends to encourage short-term thinking.

Return on Investment

Return on investment (ROI) is probably the most well-known financial measurement technique, being fairly easy to calculate but still very meaningful. It divides the total dollars in expected return by the initial investment, and the resulting answer is expressed in terms of *percent*. This is important to remember, so you don't embarrass yourself by saying something like, "Your return on investment is one million dollars."

To calculate ROI for a series of expected cash flows over several years, use the following formula:

$$\text{Lifetime ROI} = (\text{Total expected cash flows} - \text{initial investment}) \div \text{initial investment}$$

This calculation yields a ratio that tells the decision maker the percentage of total benefit over the life of the investment relative to the amount of the investment. To get a more meaningful figure, divide the lifetime ROI by the expected useful life of the asset in order to arrive at an *annualized* ROI (sometimes called AROR: annualized rate of return). Investment returns are always expressed in terms of the annualized interest rate (at least when you are not trying to confuse the consumer—maybe that is why credit-card interest rates are expressed in monthly percentages). The simplest way to do this is to add the cumulative cash inflows and divide the total by the number of years, which will give you the average annual cash benefit.

Let's take a look at our worksheet in Figure 15-1 to illustrate these points:

- Cumulative cash inflow, years 1–5: $737,900
- Initial investment: $250,000
- Lifetime ROI: (737,900 − 250,000) ÷ 250,000 = 1.95 = 195%
- Annual ROI: (487,900 ÷ 5) ÷ 250,000 = 0.39 = 39%

Both calculations, lifetime and annualized ROI, may be useful. For example, suppose you have an investment that will generate $50,000 in annual benefits but will fall apart after two years; an alternative investment of the same amount will generate $40,000 in annual benefits but will last four years. The first investment will have a higher annual ROI but a lower lifetime ROI. Which one is considered a more attractive investment depends on the goals and needs of the buyer. Some may prefer more cash up front even if the total benefit is lower.

Your customer might have specified a *hurdle rate*, which is an interest rate that any investment must exceed if it is even to be considered. You should find out the customer's hurdle rate as soon as possible in the sales process. Often the hurdle rate is the company's cost of capital. Obviously, it can never be lower than the cost of capital because then the company would lose money on any investment that just meets the hurdle rate.

Using ROI is a very popular method because it has several distinct advantages:

- It is easy to calculate and easy to understand.
- It is useful for comparing investments of different amounts.
- The resulting answer can be compared with the company's cost of capital. In theory, any investment that exceeds the company's cost of capital is worth making, because it will add profits to the bottom line. Any investment that does not exceed the company's cost of capital is a money loser, even if it appears on the surface to generate positive cash flow.

However, ROI does have some drawbacks. It does not distinguish by size of investment, so a large investment returning huge amounts of cash flow to the company may suffer in comparison with a much smaller investment. Good common sense on the part of your buyers dictates that this is not too much of a disadvantage. Where ROI does come up short is in failing to account for the time value of money. For this, we need to use discounted cash flow techniques.

Discounted Cash Flow Techniques

Discounted cash flow techniques are used because a dollar today is worth more than a dollar tomorrow, and investments that generate returns long into the future must take this into account. Before we introduce the most common techniques, it is necessary to review two concepts: the time value of money and cost of capital.

Time Value of Money

Which would you rather have: $100 handed to you today, or $100 handed to you next year? Obviously, you would rather have the money today, because you can use it immediately. More important,

$100.00	$110.00	$121.00	$133.10
Today	1 Year	2 Years	3 Years

Figure 15-2.   Future-Value Timeline

you can put it to work for you to earn an additional return. Since money can be invested to make more money, there is a *time value* associated with it. The sooner you receive it, the more it is worth. Additionally, a precise value can be assigned to the passage of time. To illustrate these two points, let's look at the timeline in Figure 15-2.

If you were able to put your money into a savings account that paid 10 percent, and leave it in there for three years, the timeline shows how much money you would have in the account at the end of each year. One hundred dollars plus 10 percent equals $110; plus 10 percent equals $121, and so on.

Because the timeline shows how much a dollar invested today will be worth in the future, it is called a *future-value timeline*. To make the timeline a useful tool for investment decisions, we need to work backward along it. Instead of figuring out what a dollar will be worth in the future, we need to figure out what a dollar received in the future is worth today. We do this using a *present-value timeline* as shown in Figure 15-3.

The present-value timeline answers the following question: "How much do I have to invest today in order to have $100 in one year, two years, and so on?" In other words, if I know I will receive $100 at this time next year, that would be equivalent to receiving $90.91 today, assuming that I could invest my funds at 10 percent. According to this timeline, $90.91 is the discounted value of $100 received a year from now, assuming a return of 10 percent. If you had to wait three years to receive your money, you would just as soon choose to receive $75.13 today as $100 in three years.

$100.00	$90.91	$82.64	$75.13
Today	1 Year	2 Years	3 Years

Figure 15-3.   Present-Value Timeline

As you can see, timing makes a significant impact on the value of an investment. All things being equal, an investment that generates returns sooner than another is preferable.

Cost of Capital

Similarly, the rate at which money can be invested makes a difference. If you change the cost of capital employed in the preceding timelines to 5 percent, $100 invested today would be worth only $105 in a year; and $100 received a year from now would be worth $95.23 today. If you change the cost of capital to 15 percent, then $100 in one year would be worth only $86.96. Therefore, the higher the cost of capital, the greater the amount of discount in the value of money.

These calculations are necessary because money is not free. The companies you are selling to have many different alternatives for employing their funds, and most of these will generate returns far into the future. That means that in order to purchase your product, they must give up something else: the returns that could have been generated by using that cash for something else, even if only to pay off debt. For a cash-poor customer, the cost may be the interest rate the company must pay to borrow the funds to purchase your solution. Even for a cash-rich customer, those funds are not free. At a minimum, the cost of capital would be the expected return on another investment of equal risk.

Cost of capital is dependent on several variables, including the general level of interest rates in the economy and the condition of the company's own balance sheet. Cash-poor companies may have to borrow funds to purchase your product, which would require that you generate higher returns to compensate. As a salesperson, you have no control over either of these factors, but you may be able to control the third variable: risk.

The cost of capital of an investment is highly dependent on the risk inherent in the investment. U.S. Treasury bonds pay much lower interest rates than "junk" bonds, which are unsecured obligations of highly leveraged companies. Investors are willing to accept the lower returns of Treasuries, however, because their money is safer, and the probability of being repaid is much higher. The same goes for purchasing decisions. When your customers are buying new products or unproved technologies, they will expect much higher returns to compensate for the higher perceived levels of risk. As we saw in previous chapters, you may have some measure of control over the level of risk perceived by your customers.

Discounted Cash Flow Measurements

The two principal financial measurement techniques that factor in the time value of money are net present value and internal rate of return.

Net Present Value (NPV)

The NPV applies a discount factor to each expected return to compute how much it is worth in today's dollars, adds them all up, and subtracts the amount of the investment. Referring back to Figure 15-1, we see that the initial investment of $250,000 is subtracted from the present values of each of the next five years' expected cash flows. The answer is expressed in terms of dollars. Because the cost of capital is factored in, an NPV greater than zero means that the investment will return greater than the cost of capital. Theoretically, then, any investment with a positive NPV will add value to the firm. In real life, however, that NPV will be compared with alternative solutions and even with other uses for the funds unrelated to your product line.

Net present value is a very powerful and useful technique because it allows the decision maker to factor in the cost of capital, risk of the investment, and timing of the expected cash flows, so it is a very commonly used measuring stick. Its principal drawback is that it makes it difficult to compare investments of different amounts. There are two ways to get around this shortcoming. Probably the more common is the internal rate of return.

Internal Rate of Return (IRR)

If you were to try different interest rates in the NPV calculation, you would see that higher costs of capital result in lower NPVs. Beginning with a positive NPV, you would find that if you raised the rates high enough, the NPV would be exactly zero. The rate at which the NPV equals zero is the internal rate of return. The IRR is useful because it yields an answer in the form of an interest rate, which makes it easier to compare that investment against others of different amounts.

Profitability Index

The other alternative, the profitability index, divides the net present value by the initial investment. The resulting ratio makes it easy to compare investments of different amounts. In our example, the profitability index is 1.08, which is pretty high.

Which Technique Do You Use?

As you can see from the preceding discussion, there are a number of measurement techniques that may be used by your customers. This chapter has presented only the most common ones. Each has certain disadvantages and advantages, and no one technique will definitively point out the best investment choice from the customer's point of view. Most financial proposals use several techniques at once in order to cover all the bases and biases, but probably the best thing to do is to ask your customers which method they prefer or require by policy.

However, since different techniques may yield different answers regarding the best alternative for a customer, your goal as a salesperson is to gain agreement on the relevant measurement techniques that will favor your solution. Suppose that your solution costs more and takes longer to implement but will yield greater profits or a longer term than your competitor's solution. Your payback period will be much longer than the competitor's solution, but the IRR will be higher. Obviously, your goal is to encourage your customer to look beyond the short-term disadvantage and take the long-term view.

The key to doing this successfully is to start early. If you wait until the proposals are done and then try to argue for the results that support you, you may have trouble. You must know enough about your solution, the competitors' solutions, and your customer's needs in order to shape the customer's thinking early in the process in the direction that plays to your strengths. You can bet that the competitors will be doing the same thing; that is why knowledge is your best weapon and your best defense.

16

A Final Word

Education is what remains after you've forgotten everything you've learned.

Albert Einstein

There is a lot of information packed into the pages of the book you have just read. It would be absurd to expect that you will remember everything as you put this book down and continue your sales efforts. By now you have seen that the way to partnering with your customers to improve their competitive advantage is not easy. The intimate knowledge of your customers that partnering demands takes time to acquire and develop. That's exactly why you should do it! Because it's so hard to do, those who make the effort will stand out and will be rewarded.

Even if you still have trouble keeping straight in your mind the difference between gross profits and operating profits (and you can always refer back to this book when you need it), if you keep three important ideas in mind, you will definitely see a difference in your approach to your customers—and in your success.

First, let your actions be guided by a genuine concern and care for the success of your customers. Unless you care about your customers, the techniques described in this book can quickly become barren (and boring) exercises in number crunching. If you truly get excited about what makes your customers excited, and the factors that contribute to their success, you will have no problem with the occasional calculation you must do. The neat thing about this type of selling is that once you really get to know your customers, it's hard not to get emotionally involved with their achievements and success. You will soon find yourself talking about "us" instead of "you," and your customers will too.

The next requirement follows from the first: be curious. Be inquisitive, learn all you can about your customers and their industries, and about business in general. This requirement should not be too onerous, because the more you learn about your customers and their industries, the easier it will be to sustain and stoke your curiosity. You will find it much more rewarding than dry knowledge of your specific product, and you will become much more interesting for your customers to talk to as a result.

Finally, to paraphrase a wise and very successful old banker of my acquaintance, "To succeed in business, you only have to know how to do four things well: add, subtract, multiply, and divide." In other words, the concepts we have explored in this book are not difficult; they boil down to plain common sense, which may turn out to be an uncommon virtue when dealing with your customers.

Index